REI Editions

All our ebooks can be read on the following devices:
- Computer
- eReader
- iOS
- Android
- Blackberry
- Window
- Tablet
- Mobile phone

Cloaks - Brown - Kittel - Graf

The Focke-Wulf FW 190

ISBN: 9782372973250

Published: November 2015
New edition completely revised and updated: January 2025
Copyright © 2015-2025 REI Editions
www.rei-editions.com

Mantelli - Brown - Kittel - Graf

The Focke-Wulf FW 190

REI Editions

Index

Focke Wulf FW 190 9
    History 12
    Technique 40
    Technical Features 47
    MG 131 machine gun 48
    MG 151 cannon 49
    Use 51
BMW 801 Engine 57
    Technical features 61
    Versions 62
Fw 190 V 66
Fw 190 A 69
    A-0 69
    A-1 71
    A-2 73
    A-3 75
    A-4 78
    A-5 81

- A-6 85
- A-7 88
- A-8 91
- A-9 94

Fw 190 B and C 95

Fw 190 D 98

Fw 190F 103

Fw 190 G 110

Fw Ta 152 113

- Technical Features 120
- Versions 121

Focke Wulf Ta 154 123

- Technical Features 125

Hans Hahn 126

Gerhard Barkhorn 129

Heinz Sachsenberg 133

Focke Wulf FW 190

The Focke-Wulf Fw 190 was a single-seat, single-engine, low-wing monoplane fighter/bomber developed by the German aircraft manufacturer Focke-Wulf in the 1930s and used by the Luftwaffe during the Second World War.
- At the time of its entry into service in 1941, it was, in the opinion of some authors, the most advanced fighter in the world.

The German fighter's high wing loading was the cause of one of its defects, its tendency to stall without warning during high-g turns, due to elastic deformation of the wingtips, resulting in inversion and spin, which was difficult to remedy if the altitude was too low.
- Faster than the Spitfire, its roll rate was exceptional.

It underwent continuous development and improvements which allowed it to remain competitive with the most modern Allied aircraft until Germany's surrender in May 1945: it was generally considered by pilots to be superior to the other main German fighter, the Messerschmitt Bf 109.
- In dozens of versions, the Fw 190 was built in 13,367 examples as an interceptor and 6,634 as a fighter-bomber and distinguished itself on all fronts.

The inspiring concept of the Fw 190 was to create a relatively simple aircraft, which could be used alongside the Messerschmitt Bf 109 in fighter squadrons, but which would have substantially better performance than the Augusta-based fighter.

The technical body of the German Air Force had requested a speed of 640 km/h at 4,000 meters: this unprecedented requirement required an extreme design commitment, aimed at the simultaneous search for power, speed and compactness.

- It was equipped with both radial and inline engines.

It had no problems maneuvering up to over 600 km/h and, therefore, could fight easily even at high speed, then disengage by escaping the Spitfire in dizzying dives.
When it came to climbing by speed, the mass of the FW-190 allowed it to easily leave the Spitfire behind: in climbing, the FW-190 beat all aircraft except the Spitfire Mk IX.

- The only problem was the stall, which reached 204 km/h and came on furiously, almost overturning the wing of the plane, although recovery was possible and easy, by giving more engine.

Since the FW-190 was not too keen on fighting unless at high speed, this was less of a problem, while at low altitude, on landing, the aircraft stalled at less than 170 km/h and this time gave the pilot ample warning, which was necessary because otherwise there would have been no time to get out.
Otherwise it was an exceptional aircraft, even if a little heavy in structure and wing loading.
The aircraft was one of the fruits of the genius of a famous aeronautical designer, Kurt Tank, who managed to summarize in the happiest way all the "summa" of aerodynamic and structural knowledge of the time in a project that was both classic in its general architecture and innovative in its solutions.
Indeed, the latest piston-engined fighters produced in the world, from the Soviet La.11 to the English «Sea Fury», explicitly reveal their lineage from the German pioneer.

Its small size and remarkable maneuverability were ideal for a fighter aircraft, as was the high visibility provided by the cockpit.

It was remarkably robust and the wide-track undercarriage allowed it to operate even on makeshift runways.

It took two years before the Allies were able to develop aircraft capable of competing with the Focke-Wulf, which remained, throughout the Second World War, a benchmark for Allied fighters in its various evolutions.

History

The Fw 190 was developed following a contract from the Reichsluftfahrtministerium in 1937; Kurt Tank submitted two proposals:
- One with a liquid-cooled Daimler Benz DB 601 engine.
- The other powered by the brand new air-cooled BMW 139 18-cylinder radial.

The choice fell on the radial engine, perhaps also because it was believed that Daimler-Benz production would be entirely absorbed by the aircraft that already mounted it, and in July 1938 the team of technicians, headed by Kurt Tank, and composed of around ten elements, including Rudolf Blaser, project manager, Ludwig Mittelhuber, Willi Käther and Andreas von Fählmann, began a detailed study of it.

The inspiring concept of the Fw 190 was to create a relatively simple aircraft with which to flank the Messerschmitt Bf 109 in fighter squadrons, but which was equipped with substantially better performance than those of the Augusta-based fighter.

The technical body of the German Air Force had requested a speed of 640 km/h at 4,000 meters: this unprecedented requirement required an extreme design commitment, aimed at the simultaneous search for power, speed and compactness.

After an initial order for four prototypes, their work progressed quickly, and by autumn 1938 a wooden mock-up was ready and construction of the first prototype had begun.

The Fw 190 V-1 (V for 'Versuchs', experimental) was flown on 1 June 1939 in Bremen by Captain Hans Sander, chief test pilot of Focke Wulf.

This example was powered by a 1,550 hp BMW 139 radial engine, with two 9-cylinder stars each, which drove a 330 cm

diameter VDM three-bladed propeller, contained in a characteristic aerodynamically shaped annular spinner, through which the air used to cool the engine passed.
However, reliability problems with the originally planned engine, which was prone to fires, forced Kurt Tank to revise the project in order to adopt the more voluminous 14-cylinder BMW 801.

Due to the increased weight of the engine, the airframe and landing gear were strengthened, and the cockpit was moved back: the vertical rudder was enlarged and equipped with a ground-adjustable corrector flap. The aircraft made its first flight in early winter 1940.
A performance comparison with the V-1 prototype revealed that the increased weight had led to a deterioration in flight characteristics, which would have further deteriorated with the installation of armament and military equipment.
It was necessary to redesign the wing to restore the original flight characteristics.

- This was done by increasing the span from 9.51 to 10.51 metres and the wing area from 15 m2 to 18.3 m2, and by moving the leading edge further forward.

Also planned was the adoption of a new, larger (3.65 metres) horizontal empennage and the moving forward of the vertical one.

This involved a number of changes, including strengthening the structure and moving the cockpit aft, but it also solved a problem of centre of gravity, as well as the discomfort caused to the pilot by exhaust fumes and overheating caused by the engine being too close to the cockpit.

However, this new engine also proved difficult to develop; the solution to the problems encountered took a long time, delaying the introduction of the aircraft into service.

In March 1941, the experimental unit Erprobungsstaffel 190 was formed at Rechlin, with personnel from II/JG26 and commanded by technical officer Otto Bahrens: this unit received six A-0s, with which it began a series of tests to experiment with the aircraft in operational use.

- However, the problem of engine overheating still arose, which occurred mainly on the ground and at low engine speeds, when the air flow was not yet sufficient to ensure adequate cooling, especially to the rear cylinder bank.

Problems also arose with the sophisticated automatic engine control system (Kommandogerat), fuel and lubricant leaks occurred, and the spark plugs showed abnormal wear.

The constant-speed VDM propeller also had problems, the engine panels had faulty locks and tended to open in flight, while the canopy was difficult to release above 250 km/h, due to aerodynamic pressure.

These serious drawbacks put the continuation of the program in doubt, which continued only after about 50 modifications, when the RLM approved the entry into service of the aircraft in operational departments.

As mentioned, the first prototype, designated Fw 190 V1, left the factory in May 1939 and the first flight took place on June 1, 1939, in Bremen, under the command of Caoitano Hans Sander. A second aircraft, the Fw 190 V2, flew in October 1939, armed with two 13 mm (0.51 in) MG 131 and two 7.92 mm (0.31 in) MG 17 machine guns.

- After abandoning the third and fourth prototypes, the Fw 190 V5 with the new BMW 801 engine was completed in early 1940.

Shortly afterwards, in the same year, the aircraft was fitted with wider wings, one metre longer than the original, which measured 9.5 metres, and although 10 km/h slower, this aircraft, designated Fw 190 V5g, was more manoeuvrable and had a higher climb speed than the previous model, with shorter wings, designated Fw 190 V5k.

- The first pre-production batch of Fw190A-0 aircraft consisted of thirty aircraft, nine with short-span wings and twenty-one with wider span ones.

The aircraft finally entered service in 1941, and immediately showed its potential, operating against British fighters over occupied France.

The A-2 version began to enter service in the same unit at Le Bourget from July 1941, and was produced between October 1941 and July 1942 in 952 units, divided between the Focke Wulf factories in Marienburg, the AGO in Oschersleben and the Arado in Warnemünde.

- This version boasted a top speed of 614 km/h, slightly higher than that of its best opponent, the Spitfire V.

The first official combat between Fw 190s and RAF fighters took place over the English Channel coast on 27 September 1941, and was supported by 6ª Gruppe of Jagdgeschwader 26: four Fw 190A-1s from this unit made a surprise attack on a numerically superior force of Spitfire Vs over Dunkirk, shooting down three of them without losses.

Fw 190 A-8

But there had been previous clashes (at least three) during which German pilots claimed six Spitfires shot down, including one over Dunkirk on 14 August (losses not all admitted by the opposing side), classified by the RAF as combats against unknown enemy aircraft.
- These early battles highlighted a marked superiority of the German aircraft in combat.

In particular, the Fw190 boasted a greater speed in diving and in horizontal flight, which allowed the German pilots to interrupt the battle by disengaging whenever they wanted:

The roll rate was also exceptional, thanks to highly efficient ailerons.
- The Spitfire, on the other hand, had a better ability to turn sharply.

From combat use it turned out that the Fw 190A was very effective when fighting took place at altitudes below 7,000 metres, but, above that, the efficiency of the BMW 801 engine began to decline: interventions to overcome this insufficiency began with the modification of three Fw 190A-1s.
The first one was fitted with wider wings, the cockpit was pressurised and the engine was equipped with a power booster, while the other two had standard wings but armament of two 20 mm MG 151 cannons and two 7.92 mm MG 17 machine guns.
- However, these prototypes did not achieve the expected results.

Adolf Galland's JG 26 had received its first A-1s in November 1941, while A-2s would arrive in the following months for Captain Joachim Muncheberg's II/JG26 and Captain Josef Priller's III/JG26.
These units were combat ready by January 1942, followed by I/JG26 from late March.
During this period, and precisely on 21 February 1942, the famous forcing of the English Channel took place (Operation 'Cerberus' for the Kriegsmarine, 'Donnerkeil' for the Luftwaffe) by the German naval squadron, including the heavy cruisers Scharnorst, Gneisenau and Prinz Eugen, during which the RAF supported its first major engagement with massive formations of Fw190s.
About thirty of them, together with numerous Bf109s, carried out protection cruises, with at least 16 fighters in the air at the same time, to oppose possible attacks by British bombers and torpedo bombers, and it was the Fw190 A-2s of II/JG26 that

annihilated all six Fairey Swordfish torpedo bombers, belonging to the 825th Squadron of the Fleet Air Arm, led by Lieutenant Commander Eugene Esmonde, who lost his life in that audacious and courageous, but practically suicidal attack.

- The superiority of the Fw 190 was demonstrated by JG26 in the months leading up to the summer of 1942, when its fighters enjoyed almost absolute air superiority.

For example, on June 1, eight Hurricane fighter-bombers, escorted by no less than 168 Spitfires, took part in "Circus" No. 178 over northern Belgium.

Two groups (I and III) of FW 190s scrambled to intercept them and shot down Debden's wing commander along with eight of his Spitfires, while five were damaged.

- On this occasion "Pips" Priller achieved his 73rd victory, the fifteenth with an Fw 190: JG26 suffered no losses.

The following day it was the turn of Captain Joachim Müncheberg's II Gruppe, which decimated the 403rd Canadian Squadron, which was tasked with providing air cover during a raid on St. Omer.

The Canadians lost eight of their twelve Spitfires, again without any Luftwaffe losses. After JG26, it was JG2's turn to equip themselves with the new fighter: this wing was deployed geographically to the left of the first, covering the sector from the Somme westwards over the Atlantic.

The conversion began in early March 1942, starting with Captain Hans Hahn's III/JG2 based at Théville and Morlaix (but with A-1s), at the end of April with Captain Karl Heinz Greisert's II Gruppe, which deployed its A-2s to Beaumont-le-Roger and Triqueville, and a month later with Captain Eric Leie's I/JG2, with his A-2s to Maupertus, Morlaix and St. Brieuc.

The Geschwaderstab, under the command of Lieutenant Colonel Walter Oesau, had to wait until August to exchange its Bf 109Fs for Focke Wulfs.

JG1, deployed to the right of JG26, responsible for the defence of the Dutch and German North Sea coastline, also began conversion in March, with II/JG1 becoming operational with the new fighter the following May, based at Woensdrecht and Katwik, Holland.

III and IV/JG1 converted in July, so that by the second half of 1942 the Luftwaffe had three fighter wings fully equipped with the Focke Wulf 190 on the Western Front.

The month of July, however, saw the entry onto the scene of the British Spitfire IX, which significantly reduced the technical gap with the German fighter, and the arrival of the first formations of the American 8th Air Force.

On July 4, American Independence Day, the first American bombing raid on Northern Europe took place, carried out by 12 RAF Boston bombers with half of their crews being American.

On 30 July the first clash between Fw 190s and Spitfire IXs took place during "Circus" 200, carried out by six RAF Boston bombers, escorted by Spitfire Vs and IXs, with the objective of JG26's base at Abbeville-Drucat: one Fw 190 and 14 Spitfire Vs were shot down.

In the spring of 1942 the A-3 version made its appearance, powered by a BMW 801D-2 engine with 1,700 hp at take-off, almost identical to the A-2.

- 509 units were produced, of which 75 (Aa-3 version) were sold to Türkiye.

The new model was supplied from March 1942 to the units, starting from II/JG26, which transferred its A-2s to I Gruppe.

The Fw 190A-3 had a maximum speed of 629 km/h, as attested by flight tests carried out by the British on the example flown by Lieutenant Arnim Faber of III/JG2, which landed at Pembrey, South Wales, after a course error.

From these tests the British concluded that the Fw 190 was inferior to the Spitfire IX and Typhoon, and that the Spitfire V was capable of fighting effectively.

From mid-July, however, the A-4 version began to roll off the assembly lines of various factories, externally distinguishable by the presence of a triangular support for the antenna on the top of the fin.

It was equipped with the same engine, but with a water and methanol injection device, which brought the power to a good 2,100 hp for a few minutes in the emergency of combat, allowing a maximum speed of 670 km/h.

- For comparison, the Spitfire IX reached 657 km/h, the Typhoon 645 km/h.

The appearance of the Fw 190A-4 therefore upset the plans of the RAF, which on 19 August, when Operation "Jubilee" took place, the landing at Dieppe of an amphibious force of Canadian troops, lamented the loss of 106 aircraft, including 88 Spitfires: 59 credited to JG2, 38 to JG26 and 9 to anti-aircraft fire.

During this period, German ace Lieutenant Josef "'Sepp" Wurmheller of III/JG2, increased his fame by shooting down several RAF aircraft despite having a broken leg following an accident.

In the twelve months up to the beginning of 1943, the units on the Western Front managed to maintain air superiority over the RAF, even though many units had, in the meantime, been transferred to the Eastern Front, where Hitler, in June 1941, unleashed the invasion of the Soviet Union (Operation Barbarossa).

- Fighter Command lost 600 aircraft during this period, compared to less than 170 German aircraft.

During the same period, the Luftwaffe received approximately 1,900 Fw 190s in versions up to the A-4, while the RAF had to make do with fewer than 300 Spitfire IXs and 200 Typhoons.

In addition to fighter units based on the Western Front, during 1942 the Fw 190 was delivered to other Luftwaffe units: IV/JG5, based in Norway, was equipped with it, and then units on the Eastern Front began to be equipped with it: in Russia the first unit to be equipped with the Fw 190 was the 9th Staffel Lehrgeschwader 2 in March 1942, which received the Focke Wulf Fw 190 A-3 in the reconnaissance version.

On 10 September 1942, I/JG51 Moelders, under Captain Heinrich Krafft, received a mixed complement of A-2s and A-3s, inflicting heavy losses on the Soviet Air Force, even outclassing the new Russian Lavockin La-5 fighter.

In the next six months it also joined forces with II/JG51 (December), I/JG54 Grun Hertz, Stab/JG54, III/JG54 and IV/JG51 (the latter received its Fw190 A-4s in January 1943).

The Fw 190 also began to equip fighter-bomber and reconnaissance units: in France, Nahaufklärungsgruppe 13 (reconnaissance group) received A-4/U4 reconnaissance aircraft, while in North Africa Schlachtgeschwader 2 (attack wing) was equipped with Fw 190 A-4 Trop ground-attack fighter-bombers.

The two fighter squadrons in France also formed units for harassment purposes across the Channel, 10(Jabo)/JG2 and 10(Jabo)/JG26, with targets in the south of England.

These attacks forced the RAF to prepare a defence which involved forces disproportionate to the size of the attackers, but which was necessary because these actions caused serious damage and heavy civilian losses, also due to the limited warning given by the short alert times.

- For example, on 31 October 1942, about thirty Fw 190 A-4/U1s, each armed with 500 kg of bombs, caused severe damage at Canterbury, Kent.

At the end of 1942 a special wing was created, consisting of three Gruppen, absorbing the two Staffel Jabo of the two wings JG2 and JG26: the SchnellKampfgeschwader (SKG) 10.

It was equipped with Fw 190 A-4/U8, armed with two 20 mm MG151 cannons, in the wings, and two MG17 machine guns, capable of carrying 500 kg of bombs and two additional 300-litre drop tanks.

This unit was employed in a series of attacks on the English towns of Ashford, Rye, Eastburne, Dungeness, Hastings and the outskirts of London.

On 3 April there was an attack on Eastburne and on 9 April on Folkenstone.

On 14 April, 18 aircraft destroyed a factory at Chelmsford. The entry of the United States into the war in December 1941 led to a gradual increase in heavy bomber actions from Britain, particularly with daylight actions conducted by the Americans with their Boeing B-17s and Consolidated B-24s.

These raids began by the 8th Air Force on 17 August 1942 with a raid on Rouen, and became increasingly massive.

The first Flying Fortress shot down was thanks to Captain Conny Meyer, the new commander of II/JG26: his unit took off on 6 September 1942 to intercept a formation of 30 B-17s that were attacking the Potez aircraft factory at Meaulte.

In that action the Fw 190s avoided the escort of out-of-position Spitfire IXs and shot down two Fortresses (the first by Meyer himself), damaging virtually all the others.

But the following day, JG1, during a raid on Rotterdam, lost two fighters: one to escorting Spitfires and the second shot down by defensive fire from bombers.

All this without losses on the Allied side.

The Luftwaffe had to devise new tactics to overcome the deadly crossfire, produced by the "box" formation that the bombers held, to which the attacker was subjected when attempting to attack an aircraft by approaching it from the tail.

- In those early battles, German pilots tended to open fire too early, fooled by the bomber's size, which made it appear closer.

Subsequently, from the examination of pilots' reports on attacks conducted from various directions, it emerged that frontal attacks were the most effective for damaging and destroying a bomber, also due to the vulnerability of the pilots and the lesser effectiveness of defensive fire in the frontal arc.

Fw 190 A-8N

On 2 October JG26 also suffered its first losses at the hands of B-17s, during a new raid on Meaulte, but a week later, on 9 October, in the heaviest raid attempted by the Americans so far, with over one hundred aircraft from five different Squadrons sent against industrial targets and airfields in occupied France, it took its revenge.

- The bombers flew in "V" formations of three aircraft each and were attacked by Captain Priller's III/JG26.

Two B-17s and a B-24 were shot down, with several aircraft damaged. Further east, JG1 took a heavy toll on RAF aircraft, shooting down three Mosquitos in October, followed on 25 November by a Lancaster, shot down during a small,

experimental daylight raid on Essen and other targets in north-west Germany, carried out under cover of cloud.
- JG1 increased its training in low visibility flying, to respond to possible future threats.

In November 1942, however, Operation "Torch" was implemented, the Allied landing on the coasts of North-West Africa, and the Luftwaffe was forced, in order to ward off the threat to the southern flank of "Fortress Europe", to transfer some of its units, including a fighter section: Captain Erich Leie's I/JG2 was sent to Marseille to protect the occupation of Vichy France, while Captain Felix Bolze's II/JG2 was sent to Tunisia.
As Captain Egon Meyer's III/JG2 had already been moved from Poix to Vannes-Meuÿon, to protect the Atlantic U-boat bases, virtually only JG26 remained in the English Channel.
JG26 soon had to do without III Gruppe, which had to be re-equipped with the Bf 109.
By the end of 1942, the Fw 190 force in the Channel had been reduced to just two Gruppen: to counter the activity of British heavy night bombers, a new air combat tactic was developed from the spring of 1943.
This tactic was devised by the great Ju 88 pilot Haio Herrman and was dubbed "Wilde Sau".
It provided for the use, during moonlit nights, of day fighters, under the command of expert pilots, against night bombers.
- The fighters gathered along the path of the approaching bombers and, guided by searchlights, attacked by sight, taking care not to descend below 4,500 metres, where anti-aircraft fire would target any aircraft.

In June 1943, Jagdgeschwader 300 was formed, under the command of Herrman himself, with fighter detachments based at Bonn-Hangelar, Oldenburg and Rhein, equipped with the Fw

190 A-5/U2, while other formations were equipped with Bf 109 Gs.

Command of JG300 was subsequently passed to Lieutenant Colonel Kurt Kettner and two further squadrons were formed, JG301 under the command of Major Helmut Weinrich and JG302 led by Major Ewald Jannsen.

The "Wilde Sau" proved so effective that Herrman was hailed a national hero and promoted to commander of Jagddivision 30, which brought together all three Geschwader.

- The best days of the "Wilde Sauer" tactic were in the late summer of 1943, when at least two hundred bombers of RAF Bomber Command fell under fire from day fighters deployed at night.

With the arrival of winter, however, came the decline of this tactic, both due to bad weather and the relative poor visibility, and because the Fw 190s and Bf 109s themselves were also engaged in daytime interceptions by other units, with the efficiency of the aircraft beginning to decline in a worrying way.

At the time of the major RAF bombing raids on Berlin and Nuremberg in March 1944, the lack of success achieved by the "Wilde Sau" led to its abandonment, and a return to the more traditional tactics of radar control and interception by night fighters.

- In November 1943, on the personal instructions of Hermann Goering, Commander-in-Chief of the Luftwaffe, Sturmstaffel 1 (also called Rammstaffel) was formed, consisting entirely of volunteers who flew Fw 190 A-7/R2, A-8/R2, R7 and R8 with additional armour weighing 200 kg.

Each of them had to shoot down at least one enemy aircraft, either using normal combat tactics or by ramming the enemy bomber.

Their usual tactic was to attack the American bomber boxes from behind, arranging themselves in wedges of 10 aircraft each, and starting to fire simultaneously at the commander's signal.

- This was typically done at a range of about 350 meters with the 20 mm guns, which were accompanied within 200 meters of the target by the 30 mm guns.

In doing so, the aircraft remained in formation without attempting any evasive maneuvers, and relied on heavy armor for passive defense and the escort of two fighter Gruppen of standard Fw 190s or Bf 109s.

They were considered by the Allies as the famous Japanese suicide pilots (the Kamikaze), but their aim was not to sacrifice the life of the pilot, nor the aircraft.

After initial successes, the Staffel was transformed into a Gruppe (IV/JG3) commanded by Major Wilhelm Moritz.

In March 1944 a new Rammstaffel was formed, based at Quedlimburg, which soon expanded to form II Sturm/JG4, led by Major Hans Gunther von Kornatski and equipped with Fw 190 A-8/R7 and R8.

- Later, other units were formed, such as the II Sturm/JG300 of Major Kurt Peters and the IV Sturm/JG300 of Major Ofterdingen.

During the USAAF bombing of Leipzig on 7 July 1944, Moritz's unit destroyed 24 B-24s in two minutes over Oschersleben, while II/JG300 destroyed nine B-17s and B-24s over Halberstadt, with the loss of only two Fw 190s, thus proving that the tactic was not at all suicidal.

Moritz was decorated with the Knight's Cross eight days later, but in November he had to give up his command, exhausted: later he obtained the command of IV/ErgJG1, still equipped with Focke Wulfs.

IV/JG3 and II/JG300 were sent to northern France soon after the Normandy landings on 6 June 1944.

It is estimated that by the end of 1944, when this tactic was abandoned, the three Sturmgruppen had shot down around 550 four-engined aircraft, with the loss of 170 pilots.

After five months of operations over France and the Netherlands, on 27 January 1943 the 8th Air Force began daylight raids on German soil, which until now had been attacked mainly at night by British RAF bombers such as Lancasters, Halifaxes, Stirlings and Wellingtons.

Between January and April, 63% of American daylight raids were directed against U-Boat bases and factories, and Emden, Wilhelmshaven, Kiel, Hamburg, Flensburg, Lübeck and Bremerhaven were attacked.

In France, La Pallice, St. Nazaire and Brest were attacked.

The RAF, on the contrary, devoted only 30% of its efforts against these types of targets, having as its main priority the industrial concentrations located in the urban areas of the Ruhr, and in March it attacked Essen, Duisburg, Wuppertal and other cities.

- This different strategy was also imposed by the lower precision possible during night bombing, which made precision bombing virtually impossible.

In both cases the first months of 1943 saw a high rate of bomber losses, of the order of 3-6% for British night bombers, which clashed with "Flak" and night fighters guided by the 'Kammhuber' radar array, and even higher for American day bombers.

The Allies realized that in order to continue the bomber offensive, it was necessary to hit the German defensive system by destroying aircraft and aircraft engine factories.
- These, together with the ball bearing factories and those for the production of synthetic petrol, were placed at the top of the priority targets from April 1943.

Furthermore, on 10 June 1943, the "Pointblank" directive divided the roles of Allied bombers as follows:
- The USAAF's goal was the destruction of the German fighter, along with the industries that equipped them and enabled them to be operational.
- The RAF had the more general objective of disorganising and destroying the German aircraft industry, which however Harris, head of Bomber Command, intended to pursue by attacking the cities where its factories were located.

This Allied bomber offensive prompted the Germans to strengthen their defense of the Reich, diverting resources from other war fronts, and by August 1943 six Jagdgruppen were under the command of the Befehlshaber Mitte (European Central Command) equipped with approximately 200 Fw 190A-4s and A-5s.
I and II/JG2, based on the Channel coast, had been nicknamed the Abbeville Boys by the Allies, and were understandably respected, and feared, by American day bomber crews.
On the Russian front, there were six other Gruppen equipped with the Fw 190, the IV/JG5, the I and III/JG51, the I, II and IV/JG54 Grunhertz, as well as other Staffel.
The increase in air defense bore fruit: on August 17, 1943, exactly one year after the first B-17 mission in Europe, the Eighth Air Force attacked Regensburg and Schweinfurt with large formations of day bombers, and the Luftwaffe scrambled

more than three hundred Fw 190s and Bf 109s to counter them, which shot down sixty bombers and damaged about a hundred.
- On 14 October the USAAF renewed its attack on Schweinfurt, and suffered an even heavier defeat, suffering the loss of 79 bombers shot down and 121 damaged, out of 228 launched.

On these occasions the 21 cm rockets with which the Fw 190A-5/R6s of JG1 and JG26 were armed were put to good use.
From these defeats the Americans drew the conclusion that it was no longer the time to send the bombers into action without an adequate fighter escort, and they made every effort to provide them with one as soon as possible.
Meanwhile, since October 1943 the 15th Air Force had joined the 8th, starting from bases in Puglia, occupied after the capitulation of Italy on September 8th.
In the winter of 1943-44 Germany had concentrated 68% of its fighters and 70% of its flak on the defense of the homeland, and the successes achieved in the autumn of 1943 against American heavy bombers left room for some optimism about the success of the air defense.
In particular, on 1 January 1944, 1,650 single- and twin-engine fighters were deployed on Western airfields, mostly in Germany, while in the Mediterranean and the Balkans there were 365, and 425 on the Russian Front.
Fighter production continued at a high level, with 725 Bf 109s and 325 Fw 190s produced by July 1943, despite bomber raids, thanks to an efficient decentralisation plan.
Fuel supplies were excellent, with synthetic fuel factories at full production.
The schools churned out new crews, although the quality level was no longer up to that of the RAF and the USAAF.
As far as flying material was concerned, the Messerschmitt Bf 109G and the Fw 190 were still a match for the Allied fighters,

and the latter also equipped the Schlachtgruppen, replacing the Ju 87D.

The Heinkel He 219 night fighter and the Junkers Ju 188 bomber had entered service, most of the problems that had plagued the early Heinkel He 177 bomber and the Messerschmitt Me 410 heavy fighter had been solved, and the revolutionary Messerschmitt Me 262 was imminent.

- But in February 1944 came the turning point that was to definitively break the balance of power in the air war: American bomber raids were now escorted by fighters right over their targets, in the heart of the Reich.

The P-38s, P-47s and P-51s, whose range had been increased, accompanied the bombers on the entire outward and return journey, drastically reducing the successes achieved by the German fighters.

By April, the U.S. Eighth Air Force had virtually achieved air superiority, and bombers were causing severe damage to aircraft factories.

In July 1944, to face the emergency, the Germans decided to concentrate their efforts on the production of fighter planes, implementing a plan to decentralize the industries, to make them less vulnerable to air attacks.

The availability of fighters thus increased again, reaching 2,995 examples delivered in September, of which 1,605 Bf 109s and 1,390 Fw 190s.

In the meantime, however, the Allies had begun to attack the fuel production industries, and for this task, on 5 April 1944, the 15th Air Force, based in Foggia attacked the oil fields of Ploesti, Romania, which were also threatened from the ground by the advancing Soviets: the 8th Air Force in turn attacked oil targets on 12, 28 and 29 May.

These attacks were halted by Overlord, the Normandy landings, which took place on 6 June, and were resumed by the 8th Air Force, which attacked synthetic fuel factories at Leuna, Politz, Böhlen, Lutzkendorf, Magdeburg, Zeitz and Ruhland, which produced 40% of Germany's fuel needs.

German fuel reserves, which in September 1943 amounted to 280,000 tons, and which had reached 574,000 tons in April 1944, including the Fuhrer's reserve, began to run low from August 1944 due to the Allied offensive.

In fact, the production went:
- From 195,000 tons in May
- At 52,000 in June
- At 35,000 in July
- At 16.000 in August
- Only 7,000 in September.

In August 1944, attacks by the 15th Air Force were also renewed against the oil fields of Ploesti, Brux and others, which were then captured by the Soviets at the end of the same month.
- The Luftwaffe was about to be defeated on the ground rather than in the air.

But let's see what the fighter deployment was in the last year of the war: on 1 April 1944 the Luftwaffe had 1,675 Bf 109s and Fw 190s, of which 850 were assigned to the Defense of the Reich against the offensive of the 8th and 15th American Air Forces.

In northern France and Belgium, only 135 fighters were available to face attacks by the US 9th Air Force and RAF Fighter Command.

In Norway there were 40 Fw 190s of IV/JG5, while in Italy there were 145 Bf 109s of JG53 and JG77.

On the Eastern Front there were only 515 fighters to cover a 1,500 km front against the new, numerous Russian Yakovlev Yak-9D and Lavochin La-7 fighters.

It was planned to reinforce the deployment in France in the event of an Allied landing by drawing units from the Reich Defence Force.

In particular, on 31 May, fighter forces in the west consisted of Major Kurt Bühligen's JG2, with I and III/JG2 equipped with Fw 190A-8s, the Geschwaderstab and II/JG2 with a mixed force of Fw 190A-8s and Bf 109Gs, and "Pips" Priller's JG26, with the Geschwaderstab, I, II and III/JG26 on Fw 190A-8s.

There were also 73 fighter-bombers available in III/SG4 and I/SKG10.

These units were however dispersed throughout the territory of France.

The day of the invasion, the incursion of the two Fw 190s of Jasef Priller and his wingman on the landing beaches remained famous, a testimony to the scarcity of the German reaction, and in fact the Luftwaffe was able to oppose only 100 fighter sorties and 170 bomber sorties against the total of 14,674 of the Allies.

In the 36 hours following the invasion, 200 Fw 190s and Bf 109s were sent as reinforcements.

On 10 June 1944, the following fighter units were based in France: Stab, I, II and III/JG1, II, III and IV(Sturm)/JG3, I/JG5, I, II and 10/JG11, STab, I, III and IV/JG27, II/JG53 and III/JG54.

Also present was the autonomous group JGr 200, formed with training aircraft, which however did not take part in the operations in Normandy. After only ten days, five fighter groups had to be withdrawn to Germany for rest.

For example, on 25 June, at 1pm, II/JG1 was strafed by 16 P-51s, suffering the loss of 15 of its 24 Fw 190s, and was out of action for several days: JG26 lost 67 pilots between D-Day and 31 August.

By that date, the defeats of the Wehrmacht on the ground, culminating in the encirclement of many German soldiers in the Falaise pocket, led to a gradual withdrawal of the Luftwaffe fighter units to their bases in Germany, including the JG2 and JG26 wings, which had, until then, been the defensive bulwarks in the defence of France.

Fw 190 A-8

With the resumption of the Allied offensive against the synthetic fuel industries, the fighter contingent on the Western Front was reduced to just 300 aircraft in September 1944, and that on the Eastern Front to 375, while 1,260 were deployed for the defense of the Reich.

It was, therefore, a respectable force, even if deprived of the contribution of the many veterans who had disappeared during the conflict, replaced by inexperienced pilots, even if animated by a strong fighting spirit.

- The flying material was good, consisting largely of the Messerschmitt Bf 109G-14 and K-4, and the Focke Wulf Fw 190A-8, A-9 and D-9.

The "Dora", FW 190D, was delivered to III/JG54 of Captain Robert Wieiss, the first unit to be equipped with one, and from 12 October 1944 it was tasked with protecting the airfields of Kommando Nowotny, the Messerschmitt Me 262A jet fighter unit, the first of the Luftwaffe.

The inexperience of the German pilots led to real carnage: during the raid on Leuna on 2 November 1944 seventy pilots were killed and 28 were wounded, even if the destruction of 30 B-17s and 7 Mustangs was claimed.

Similar losses occurred on the 21st and 26th of the same month, and after that forces were saved for the Ardennes Offensive, the Wehrmacht's last on the Western Front.

This offensive, whose main objective was the conquest of the port of Antwerp, with the consequent separation between British and American troops, with the annihilation of the former in a pocket (almost a smaller-scale re-edition of the 1940 offensive), was launched on 16 December 1944, protected by terrible weather conditions.

In this offensive, around one hundred Fw 190s transferred from Luftflotte 6 on the Eastern Front were also employed in the ground attack.

- In total, 1,770 aircraft were used, including Fw 190s and Bf 109s, while 400 remained in defense of the German Reich.

By 17 December, the Schlachtgruppen had flown 600 sorties, mostly against Allied lines of communication.

The last days of the year saw the failure of the German offensive, due both to the lack of fuel and to an improvement in the weather, which allowed the Allied air force to unleash all its power to stop the offensive attacks of the German aircraft.

- With the situation on the ground now compromised, on 1 January 1945 the Luftwaffe launched Operation Bodenplatte, a surprise low-level attack by around 900 Fw 190s and Bf 109s against Allied airfields in Belgium and the Netherlands.

Among the targets chosen were Eindhoven, St. Denis-Westrem, Volkel, Evere, Grimberghen, Melsbroek, Antwerp-Duerne, St. Trond, Le Culot, Asch and Metz-Frascaty.

Despite the success of the attack, the German units had to suffer a tragic decimation at the hands of their own anti-aircraft units. In total, the losses were 170 killed or missing in action, 67 prisoners and 18 wounded, against the destruction of 144 RAF aircraft, 134 USAAF aircraft and the more or less serious damage of, respectively, 84 and 62 aircraft.

The offensive, therefore, had cost the Luftwaffe dearly, which did not have time to heal its wounds: in the meantime, the Russians had resumed pressing towards Prussia, Poland and Hungary, and on 15 January 300 aircraft were sent to the Eastern Front to reinforce the pre-existing deployment of 1,875 aircraft, while on 22 January another 500 aircraft followed.

- Among them were 650 fighters and 100 Fw 190 attack aircraft.

The fighter force on the Eastern Front was, therefore, about 850-900 aircraft, supported by about 700 ground attack aircraft.

To save forces, it was decided to commit a maximum of 50% of the fighter units to combat, keeping the remainder on the ground for rest and fuel savings, and not to pursue enemy aircraft beyond the front line.
Furthermore, any fighting that was not under the most favorable circumstances had to be avoided.

- The top priority was the defense of supply lines.

On the Eastern Front, on 6 March the Wehrmacht launched an offensive in an attempt to recapture Budapest, but the Luftwaffe was unable to provide adequate support.
The Soviets were already able to counterattack on March 16, frustrating the German attempt by reaching the border with Austria on March 28, conquering Vienna on April 13, and even surrounding Berlin by the end of the month.
Because of the deteriorating situation in the East, when the Western Allies crossed the Rhine, the Germans could only mount 200 sorties against the British and 350-400 against the Americans.
Furthermore, the fuel situation was increasingly dire, and the Allied attack on German airfields, launched on 21 March, reduced the Luftwaffe's options to a minimum.
The surviving German air forces were then desperately thrown mostly eastwards against the Soviets, with a peak effort of 1,100 sorties a day in mid-April against the troops besieging Berlin: such desperate actions ceased only with the progressive occupation of the air bases.

- Berlin capitulated on May 2, and Germany surrendered to the Allies on May 8, 1945.

A different attempt was the Fw 190 C, some examples of which were equipped with the Daimler-Benz DB 603 engine with Hirth 9-2281 turbocharger in large ventral nacelles which earned them the nickname Kanguruh.
But tests revealed that the turbocharger was unreliable and the programme was abandoned in favour of the Focke-Wulf 190 D.
Thus, at the end of 1943, several Fw 190 A-7s were modified with the installation of Junkers Jumo 213A inline engines.
The nose line was maintained by using an annular radiator inside a cowling similar to that covering the radial engine.
The modifications involved a lengthening of the rear part of the fuselage by 50 centimetres and an increase in the surface area of the tailplanes, to compensate for the 60 centimetre increase in length of the nose, due to the larger size of the engine.

Fw 190 D-9

From these prototypes, designated Fw 190 D-0, was derived the production version Fw 190 D-9, popularly known as the "long-nose 190" or "Dora 9", armed with two MG 151 cannon and two

MG 131 machine guns, with a water- methanol injection system to increase, in case of emergency, the power to a good 2,240 hp. In the "D" configuration the fighter reached perhaps its best expression and approximately 700 examples were built until 1945.

The F series, in which the Fw 190 was transformed into a fighter-bomber, entered the scene at the end of 1942.

The G series machines followed.

Technique

The aircraft had an all-metal monocoque fuselage, except for the fabric-covered tailplanes.
The fuselage consisted of two sections:
- The front, which went from the firewall to the driver's shoulders.
  The anterior trunk was in turn divided into two sections:
  ❖ The upper one, delimited below by the floor of the passenger compartment, on four side members, of which the two upper ones, with a U-shaped section, also acted as guides for the sliding hood, which started from the four attachments of the engine mount.
  ❖ The lower one, whose belly was easily removable, and which housed the two self-sealing fuel tanks, with a total capacity of 524 litres.
- The rear, which from that section reached up to the tail section.
  The rear fuselage section, with a traditional half-shell structure, was connected by bolts to both the front fuselage and the tail group.

The empennage consisted of a twin-spar fin and a twin-spar stabilizer, to which the rudder and elevator were hinged.
The left side covering of the fin, between the two longerons, was removable to allow access to the tailwheel retraction mechanism and the related shock absorber, while the electrically adjustable stabilizer was made up of two left and right elements, connected by bolts on the centreline of the aircraft.
The aerodynamically and dynamically compensated movable surfaces, such as the ailerons, had small ground-adjustable corrector flaps on the trailing edge.

The FW 190 had no hydraulic system and the electrical system provided, among other things:
- The maneuver of the flaps, which could be lowered up to 58°.
- Adjusting the propeller pitch.
- The adjustment of the cylindrical sleeve which, by translating, varied the flow of air which cooled the engine.
- The retraction and lowering of the trolley.
- The operation of the on-board weapons.

The wing of the FW 190A consisted of a single element, excluding the replaceable terminals, based on the robust spar, which in the central section had a double box structure with three sheet metal cores. On the one hand this meant that if one of them was damaged both had to be replaced, on the other hand the structure was extremely robust and highly reliable.

Perpendicular to the axis of the aircraft, in the wing trunk that passed through the fuselage, the spar had a forward deflection of 14° up to the articulation of the landing gear legs, thus ensuring space for their retraction, and again perpendicular to the axis of the aircraft it then ran up to the wingtips with a double T section.

The dorsal and ventral skins consisted of four separate panels, stiffened by false ribs and stringers arranged along the opening: they were connected to each other through the front spar, the rear spar, which carried the hinges of the Frise-type ailerons and the split flaps, and five strength ribs for each half-wing.

The inner leading edge sections, into which the front landing gear legs retracted, were bolted to the main spar.

The wing control surfaces were almost all fabric-covered metal, as were the ailerons, while the slats were entirely metal.

- Visibility from the cockpit in flight was excellent, but was rather poor during taxiing due to the large size of the engine.

The windshield was bulletproof, while the pilot's shoulders were protected by 8 mm thick armor and 14 mm for the head. Also armored was the front lip of the Naca, which also served as a radiator for the lubricant.
- The sliding roof could be released, if necessary, by the action of two explosive cartridges.

The instrumentation was rationally arranged on the dashboard, and the aircraft was equipped with an oxygen inhalation system, fed by tanks placed behind the pilot: also behind the pilot was installed the radio transceiver, which could be of various models.

The armored glass was 50–55 mm at the front and 30 mm at the sides, little more than a normal windshield.

The very robust and wide-tracked trolley had wheels with a diameter of 700 mm at the front and 350 mm at the rear.

The legs were equipped with oleo-pneumatic shock absorbers, and two electric motors bolted to the wing spar controlled the retraction and lowering of the front legs, with rotation towards the aircraft's centreline, through a gear reduction system with a ratio of approximately 10,000 to 1.

The rear undercarriage was partially retracted by steel cables connecting it to the front undercarriage.

The tires were a generous 700 x 170 mm, necessary to support the considerable bulk of this device.

Aircraft powered by the BMW 801 engine continued to fly for a long time with operational and reliability limitations, due to overheating problems caused by the large amount of power packed into a very "tight" cowling.

- Forced ventilation aided this configuration by virtue of the presence of a fan rotating at 3.3 times the speed of the propeller.

Obviously this also meant a "waste" of part of the delivered power, but the solution was considered satisfactory.

Two further tanks were present in the forward fuselage for a total of over 630 litres, including the 115 mentioned above.

The wings also contained the armament, originally of two 13 mm MG131 machine guns, later two 7.92 mm caliber MG17s as well as two 20 mm Mauser MG FF cannons.

Later, the more modern MG 151/20 automatic cannons would appear, which implied a great increase in firepower: initially there were 2 then 4, while external machine guns were not always installed in order to save at least 100 kg of weight.

The armament of the "190" was, therefore, quite powerful and significantly better than the Me109, at least in most versions.

The machine guns in the nose had a caliber of 7.92 and 2,000 rounds but were later replaced by 13 mm MG 131s, which were finally available for production.

The collimator was a Revi model, standard for German fighters, with a reflection system for "instinctive" aiming, to avoid having to be distracted by complex actions or by aiming through reticle collimators, which were not very efficient against fast targets.

The Fw 190 mounted MG FF and MG 151 cannon with 620 rounds, in addition to the 2,000 7.92 mm rounds in the standard A-4 and A-5 models, but the Fw 190 A-6 replaced the MG FFs with two more MG 151s, and finally, in the A-7 (in the albeit small number of examples produced) and A-8 (on the contrary produced in large series) the MG 17 machine guns were replaced by MG 131s, to obtain greater effectiveness against armoured opponents.

In 1943-44 several Fw 190s were fitted with additional 30 mm guns, 210 mm rockets or time bombs.

The WG-21 rockets had poor accuracy and it may be surprising that weapons of this type, considered inaccurate against ground targets, hit bomber formations at a range of up to 1,000 meters, however, their task was made easier by the large number of aircraft that made up these formations.

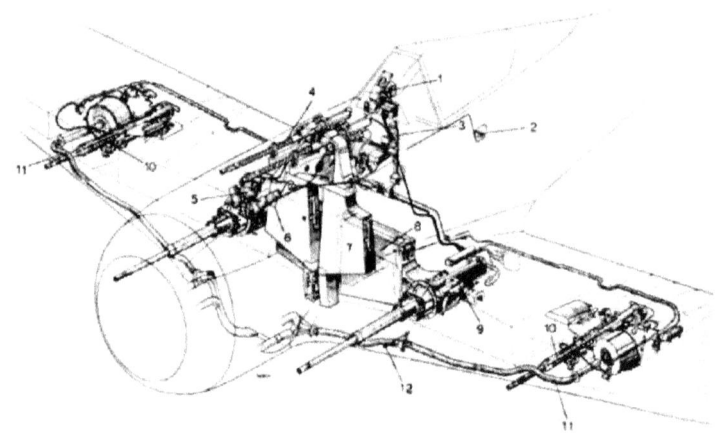

Arrangement of weapons

In the opinion of many, the FW190 was more pleasant to fly than the BF-109 and this positive impression began to emerge as soon as one sat in the cockpit, which featured a modern and rational arrangement of the instruments.

The pilot sat with his feet slightly raised, a comfortable position that allowed him to better withstand high-g maneuvers: it should be noted that the structural resistance limit of the fuselage was set at around 6g.

Leaving the landing gear and taxiing presented no problems, given the wide-track landing gear and excellent brakes, except for a certain lack of forward visibility, a typical defect of any fighter with a tricycle landing gear at the rear.

During the take-off roll, carried out with flaps at 10°, elevator trim in neutral position and propeller pitch on Auto, the aircraft had a certain tendency to bank to the left, especially if the pilot made the mistake of giving too much throttle: for this reason, many tried to taxi on three points for as long as possible, giving full throttle only when the controls reached full efficiency.

The lift-off from the runway occurred at a speed of approximately 180 km/h and, after the retraction of the landing gear and flaps, the climb began at a rate of almost 16 metres per second.

In the air the behaviour was exceptionally good and the aircraft appeared extremely docile: during flight there was no need to adjust the aileron trim, also because this possibility was missing, the trim being adjustable only on the ground.

- The ailerons were very light and maintained this characteristic from the stall speed, 204 km/h, up to approximately 645 km/h, then progressively hardening.

The elevators, however, were quite heavy at all speeds, especially above 565 km/h, but apart from this detail the flight characteristics were excellent, with excellent acceleration, supported by other qualities, such as, for example, the ability to reverse a turn faster than any opponent or the fact that the aircraft always constituted a very stable firing platform, at any speed and with all combinations of weapons.

If we add to this the extreme robustness of the cell, capable of withstanding even considerable damage, the judgment that emerges is even more positive.

The stall speed was 204 km/h and this phenomenon occurred suddenly and without warning, with the right wing lowering violently so much that the aircraft tended to overturn: the stall during landing was very different, announced by flapping, until the right wing lowered at approximately 164 km/h.

The normal landing procedure consisted of approaching the runway at around 300 km/h, then opening the flaps by about 10° at around 250 km/h before extending the landing gear, lowering the flaps even further and then arriving on the runway at a speed of around 200 km/h.

Technical Features

Dimensions and weights
- Length: 8.95 meters
- Wingspan: 10.51 meters
- Height: 3.95 meters
- Wing area: 18.30 m^2
- Empty weight: 3,470 kg
- Maximum take-off weight: 4,900 kg

Propulsion
- Engine: BMW 801D-2 radial
- Power: 1,730 hp (1,272 kW) at 4,900 meters

Performance
- Maximum speed: 656 km/h at 6,700 meters
- Autonomy: 1,470 km
- Tangency: 10,060 meters

Armament
- Machine guns: 2 x 13 mm MG 131
- Guns: 2 or 4 20 mm MG 151

MG 131 machine gun

Conceived as a fighter aircraft equipment, in a fixed position, as a swivel gun operated by a standing gunner or remotely controlled within barbettes, it was the standard heavy machine gun of Luftwaffe aircraft during the Second World War: the Messerschmitt Bf 109 and Focke-Wulf Fw 190 fighters, the Messerschmitt Me 410 zerstörer and the Junkers Ju 88 bomber.

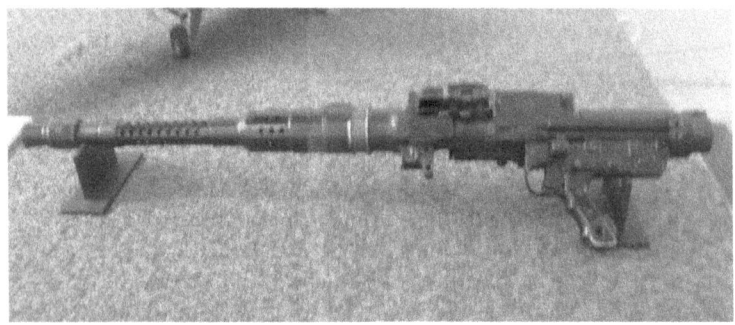

It had an electric fire mechanism that allowed it to fire through the propeller disc with minimal slowing of the rate of fire: a twin-gun version designated as the MG 131 Z was also available.
Belt-fed, air-cooled, it had a rate of fire of 930 rounds per minute with a weight of 20.5 kg and 13 mm caliber projectiles.

MG 151 cannon

The MG 151 was a 15 and later 20 mm automatic aircraft cannon developed and produced by the German company Mauser from 1940.
It was first introduced in 15 mm caliber in the Messerschmitt Bf 109F-2 in early 1941.

- According to the German classification of the time, it was considered a machine gun, even if it was equipped with explosive shells, since automatic cannons were considered as such starting from 30 mm.

Designed to replace the MG FF cannon widely used in its variants as armament of German aircraft, compared to this it had a higher rate of fire and accuracy.
It remained in use in many countries even after World War II.
From 1941 onwards, the MG 151 replaced the older and more deficient MG FF on all Luftwaffe fighters, but it was insufficient to provide the necessary firepower to the aircraft.
The German pilots, in fact, immediately realized that the impact of the 15 mm explosive shells was not sufficient and asked for larger caliber weapons.
Mauser responded by widening the neck of the 15 x 96 mm cases to 20 mm and shortening them, but increasing the length of the bullet, in order to have a greater explosive charge and greater destructive power: thus was born the 20 x 82 mm RB ammunition and the weapon designed to use it: the MG 151/20 which was, in fact, an MG 151 with a larger caliber barrel and other slight modifications, something possible thanks to the dimensions of the 20 x 82 RB cartridge being very similar to the 15 mm one.

Weight and dimensions were also very similar to the MG 151 and the two weapon models were used together throughout the conflict.

- Compared to the 15 x 96 mm ammunition, the new 20 x 82 RB offered greater impact and destructive capacity, and was immediately appreciated by German pilots.

On the other hand, it had a lower initial velocity, but not to the point of degrading ballistically, and overall both weapons proved to be modern and efficient, of high construction quality and reliability.

The old MG FF, however, remained in service, as its compactness and lightness were invaluable in the creation of the famous Schräge Musik installations, widely used on German night fighters and for which the low velocity and rate of fire did not represent a handicap.

Although adequate against enemy fighters and ground targets, the MG 151 and 151/20 proved, however, unsuitable for shooting down the heavy Allied bombers that were raging in the skies over Germany.

- The Luftwaffe found that it took an average of 25-30 hits to seriously damage a four-engined bomber, whereas the new, considerably more destructive Rheinmetall MK 103 and MK 108 30 mm guns could bring it down with only 4-5 hits.

From 1943, therefore, German fighters received the new 30 x 90 mm model, while the MG 151 - 151/20 remained standard equipment on fighter-bombers and ground-attack aircraft, as well as night fighters.

Use

Although it had been flying well before the outbreak of war, this little fighter was entirely unknown to the Allies and came as an unpleasant surprise when it was first seen flying over France in 1941.

It was, in fact, so superior to the larger and slower Spitfire V that, at first, the RAF felt it was surpassed not only numerically, but also technically.

- The first Luftwaffe unit to fly Fw 190s into combat against Supermarine Spitfires, on 27 September 1941, was 6./JG.26. The version used was the 190 A-1, with increased wingspan, 1,660 hp (1,238 kW) BMW 801C-1 radial engine, FuG 7a radio and four 7.92 mm MG 17 machine guns.

In clashes with Fighter Command fighters, however, this armament proved clearly inadequate.

This deficiency was addressed by the successor model, the Fw 190 A-2, which was equipped with two engine-mounted MG 17s and two 20 mm MG FF cannons at the wing roots, an armament that could be augmented with two more MG 17s mounted further out in the wings.

Later Fw 190A variants had an even heavier armament, with the MG FFs moved further outboard in the wings and the installation of the MG 151s, with a higher rate of fire, at the wing roots.

Armament was further enhanced with later variants of the Fw 190 A, which mounted up to six rapid-firing 20-millimeter MG 151 cannon.

Thus equipped, the Focke-Wulfs quickly gained the upper hand over the British Spitfires by virtue of their performance, which was clearly superior at the time thanks also to a more powerful engine, the BMW 801C-2.0.

- Although the Fw 190 was no match for its lightweight opponents in turns, its dive rate, acceleration and roll were superior: the two aircraft were equal only at high altitudes.

For a short time the A-1 saw action as a near-standard version, but the improved A-2 and A-3, the latter powered by the 1,800 hp BMW 801D engine, soon followed, ushering in large-scale production of the aircraft.

In June 1942 a Luftwaffe pilot mistakenly landed his intact Fw 190 A-3 in South Wales and the British discovered that the German fighter was better than they thought.

It was fast and had a very heavy armament: at that time the standard equipment consisted of two 7.92 mm MG 17 machine guns mounted above the engine, two Mauser cannons in the inner wing sections and two further 20 mm MG FF cannons in the outer sections. Very robust, it had excellent maneuverability, afforded the pilot excellent visibility and constituted an extremely small target.

Comparative tests were carried out to devise the best techniques to deal with the new German fighter: Spitfire pilots were advised, in practice, to avoid combat and maintain a high cruising speed to reduce the chances of being intercepted.

- As a method of evasion the British pilot was reminded that the Spitfire could out-turn the Fw 190, although not always, and if they spotted the enemy in time, to push the aircraft into a shallow dive.

Had the pursuit been prolonged, he would have been overtaken, but as about a mile was covered every ten seconds, such evasive action might be attempted with some hope of success.

Due to the growth of the models produced, the Fw 190 became operational not only in France, but also in the East and in the Mediterranean.

On all fronts the Fw 190 confirmed itself as the fastest and most powerful fighter for about a year, until the introduction of the Spitfire Mk.IX managed to rebalance the comparison, especially at high altitude.

- At low and medium altitude, the only aircraft that could match it on the Western Front was the Hawker Typhoon.

The Fw 190s were employed in attack actions against targets in England, with raids even in broad daylight and at very low altitude against high-value targets such as ports, factories and airfields.

On the Eastern Front, the adversaries were the Lavochkin La-5 and the Yakovlev Yak-9: the greater experience of the German pilots played an important role and the Soviet Air Force suffered significant damage. The evolution of the war situation led the Fw 190 units to fight in the Mediterranean Sea, where in the last months of the Desert War they operated from bases in Sardinia and Tunisia against the overwhelming power of the Anglo-Americans.

- The aircraft was also used as an escort fighter and fighter-bomber.

In Africa the Fw 190 sustained losses more or less comparable to its victories while many machines were destroyed or abandoned at Axis airfields for lack of fuel or spare parts.

The battlefield where the Fw 190 saw its greatest use, and its greatest successes, was undoubtedly the air defence of the homeland, since the bomber offensive forced the Germans to "play" more and more on the defensive.

The Fw 190s proved to be particularly suitable aircraft for dealing with Allied bombers, being able to count on very high firepower, great robustness and high speed.

Although inferior to the Bf 109 in high-altitude performance, the Fw 190 had better passive defense and could count on heavier armament and a standard ammunition load that was 50% greater.

During 1944, Allied fighter escorts, now able to take off from French bases liberated after the Normandy landings, had joined the bombers in striking Germany and protected them from the previously relatively easy attack action of German fighters.

The Germans, while waiting for the Fw 190 D, the Ta 152 and jets like the Messerschmitt Me 262, used the Fw 190 extensively as "destroyer" aircraft, with positive results throughout 1944, thanks to their remarkable performance, despite a further increase in weight, up to 200 kg, due to the installation of additional 5 mm thick armour.

- Not infrequently, the German Air Force deployed units of Bf 109s to "escort" the Fw 190s on their missions: these units had the task of engaging the escort fighters, thus freeing the Fw 190s to move towards the main objective.

The Fw 190s, given their greater autonomy and load capacity for weapons and radar, were also used for night hunting: initially without specific equipment, then equipped with specially prepared equipment such as Neptun radars and auxiliary radios. Various special equipment kits were prepared, suitable both for updating the various aircraft and for making them suitable for different tactical needs.

Most German pilots were skeptical of the new aircraft but when they had the chance to try it out they were very surprised.

With the "D" version the fighter reached perhaps its best expression and proved capable of competing even with the

American P-51D Mustang, for many the best fighter of the conflict.

The Fw 190 D-9, in particular, was considered by many pilots to be superior to any other aircraft of this category then employed by the Luftwaffe.

- Approximately 700 were built, but by the time it came into widespread use in early 1945, the optimum deployment of this excellent aircraft was limited by the severe shortage of jet fuel.

The aircraft of the long-range tactical bomber version G, capable of carrying bombs weighing 1,800 kg, were used to strike targets behind the front line, in all weather conditions.

Finally, the Fw 190 F, a tactical bombing version with a shorter range, was preferably intended for the Russian front, in order to counter enemy tanks: the results, often devastating, obtained initially with conventional weapons and later with the use of rockets, were however insufficient to stop the advance of the enemy armies.

Another important but unusual task performed by the Fw 190 was the defense of bases from which the early Luftwaffe jets operated.

Since these aircraft were particularly vulnerable during take-off and landing, other aircraft acted as guardians for them.

In the final stages of the conflict, the Fw 190s were assigned a variety of tasks, regardless of the role for which they had been designed, as was the case for all aircraft that remained available and capable of operation.

Soviet pilots, however, did not consider the Fw 190 an excellent aircraft in every respect.

For Nikolai G. Golodnikov, the "Fokker" (as the Russians called the Fw 190) was, yes, an extremely powerful and fast aircraft, but as a fighter it was inferior to the Bf 109.

"It did not accelerate as quickly, and in this respect was inferior to most of our aircraft, except perhaps the P-40," supplied by the Americans under the Lend-Lease program.

"The German pilots," the Soviet pilot emphasized, "preferred frontal assaults, counting on the presence of the radial engine, which acted as a shield, and on the extremely powerful armament: four 20-millimeter cannons and two machine guns. But the Luftwaffe pilots soon learned to avoid these attacks against the Bell P-39 Airacobras, also supplied by the United States, which with a single shot from their 37-millimeter cannon were capable of destroying an aircraft."

American pilot Kit Carson, an ace who would achieve several successes with the North American P-51 Mustang and an instructor of Allied fighters, defined it, contrary to the Russians, as "a fighter plane in every inch of its length".

BMW 801 Engine

The BMW 801 was a radial aircraft engine built by BMW with a double-star construction with 14 cylinders, seven cylinders each, and the system was cooled exclusively by air.

The bore and stroke were both 156 mm, resulting in a displacement of approximately 41.8 litres (2,560 in^3).

Its weight, complete with the parts that allowed it to be mounted on the aircraft, was 1,250 kg and its length varied, depending on the version, from 1.27 to 2 metres.

- The power output ranged, depending on the version, from a minimum of 1,600 hp (1,193 kW) to a maximum of 2,000 hp (1,491 kW).

The design of this engine began based on the experience gained by BMW in the 1930s with the construction, under license, of the Pratt & Whitney R-1690 Hornet, which the company had named the BMW Hornet.

An improved version, the BMW 132, was introduced, which enjoyed considerable sales success throughout the 1930s.

In 1935 the RLM financed the construction of two prototypes of large radial engines: one design had been submitted by BRAMO and another by BMW.

Subsequently, the latter purchased BRAMO, incorporating the design staff into itself and thus putting an end to the BRAMO project.

The result was a proposal for a twin-star version of the BMW 132 engine which was identified as the BMW 139: according to the design, the engine was to develop 1,400 hp (1,044 kW) of power.

This engine was initially intended for use on bombers and transport aircraft, a common use for radial engines on German aircraft.

The use of this type of engine on land-based fighters was severely limited by the large frontal section that they required and, hence, by the aerodynamic drag that this configuration generated.

It was Kurt Tank, the designer of Focke Wulf, who had the idea of using a radial engine for his future fighter, which would become the Focke-Wulf Fw 190.

Front view of a BMW 801

The idea he had to overcome the problem of resistance, and therefore be able to provide the aircraft with a sleek

aerodynamic line, was to incorporate inside the engine cowling, behind the propeller, which was equipped with a large nose cone, a fan driven by the engine itself which pushed air towards it, cooling it.
- Some of this air would be sucked in by special S-shaped ducts and conveyed to the oil radiator.

However, it was not possible to get this system to work with the BMW 139. Furthermore, this project seemed out of date, so in 1938 BMW proposed a new project that could, however, go into production quickly.

Once approval was obtained, work began the following October.

The new engine was designated the BMW 801, as BMW had been assigned a new series of numbers with which to designate engines.

The differences between the new engine, which the company called the BMW 801, and the 139 were minimal and limited mainly to details.
- The engine retained the two-valve-per-cylinder configuration, despite the fact that almost all aircraft engines at the time already used four valves or even sleeve valves, as in some English engines.

To avoid the shift in the center of gravity, the cockpit was moved back, thus solving the problem of the temperatures inside, but visibility while taxiing was drastically reduced.

To balance the increased weight and loss of agility, a new, wider-span wing was designed, restoring the wing loading: all the weight increases were balanced by the increased power of the BMW 801.

New flight tests confirmed that all problems had been resolved except the engine temperature.

Furthermore, this unit was equipped with a single-stage, two-speed centrifugal compressor, driven by the engine itself and not by a hydraulic system, as was the case on the contemporary Daimler-Benz DB 601 engine.

Naturally, several recent technological innovations were incorporated, such as the valve cooling system and the direct injection fuel system.

The most important innovation was the introduction of the Kommandogerat, an electro-hydraulic unit that significantly simplified engine management.

The Kommadogerat was a device that automatically, via an electromechanical computer, managed the fuel flow, engine rpm, propeller pitch, mixture, engine advance and compressor pressure, setting the best parameters based on the supply pressure set via the engine throttle by the pilot, and the atmospheric pressure and temperature.

- This device thus relieved the pilot of all those management tasks, leaving him to concentrate on piloting and combat.

The real weak point was the oil radiator, prone to breakages and fires in the circuits: the structure of the latter was, however, armoured, 3 mm in the first models and 6.5 in the later ones, to prevent the fighter from being easily damaged.

Finally, super-power systems were available to increase flight performance both at low altitude, through the injection of methanol and water, and at high altitude, through nitrous oxide, which assisted the engine, which was equipped with a supercharger.

These systems replaced the 115-litre rear fuselage tank.

Technical features

- Engine: 14-cylinder double star radial
- Cooling: air
- Power supply: direct injection
- Distribution: two cam rings, pushrods and rocker arms, 2 valves per cylinder, equipped with sodium insert exhaust valves
- Compressor: centrifugal, single stage and two speed
- Width: 2,006 mm
- Diameter: 1,290 mm
- Displacement: 41,744 L
- Bore: 156 mm
- Stroke: 156mm
- Compression ratio: 6.5:1
- Empty weight: 1,055 kg
- Power: 1,600 hp (1,177 kW) at take-off at 2,700 rpm

Versions

The first version of the BMW 801 was the A, 1,600 hp (1,193 kW), which underwent initial trials in April 1939, just six months after design work began.

- It was followed by version B, which was identical to version A, differing only in the direction of rotation, which was to the left.

The two versions were intended to be used together on twin-engine aircraft, thus cancelling the torque generated during flight by the rotation of the propellers and improving the aircraft's handling.

The L version, optimised for desert climates, was also developed from the A.

All three of these versions exhibited a severe cooling problem and every effort was made to resolve it.

- The next version was the C, which replaced the previous versions.

This version featured a new hydraulic control for the propeller pitch and several improvements to overcome the problem of overheating, including fins placed at the rear of the engine cowling.

With the need to use the fighter at high altitude, it was necessary to review the performance of the compressor which was no longer satisfactory.

The C-1 version, fitted to the Focke Wulf FW 190 A-1 version provided 1,550 hp (1,156 kW) at take-off which was increased to 1,600 (1,193 kW) on the C-2 version adopted by the FW 190 A-2.

- These versions were also replaced by the D version which used 96 octane fuel and not 87 octane as on the A/B/C/L versions.

The take-off power of the BMW 801 D-1 was 1,700 hp (1,268 kW) rising to 1,730 hp (1,290 kW) in the D-2 version.
The D version also adopted an injection system for a 50% water and methanol mixture, called MW 50: to be precise, 50% methanol which acted as an antifreeze, 49.5% water which increased the anti-knock power of the mixture and 0.5% Schutzöl 39, an anti-corrosion additive).

- Used by the Luftwaffe in supercharged engines, it combined the anti-knock properties of the mixture with the ability to cool mechanical components such as the compressor, valve seats and combustion chamber, obtaining a superior overall efficiency.

It was introduced via a pilot-controlled injection system directly into the compressor, also allowing the supply pressure to be increased to take advantage of additional power.
The system, extremely effective at low altitude, gradually lost efficiency at higher altitudes: in fact, the supercharging was effective only below the recovery altitude, where the compressor was able to provide a boost that, otherwise, could not be exploited, while the effects due to cooling remained effective even above the recovery altitude.

Low and medium altitude performance improved greatly and engine power rose to 2,000 hp (1,491 kW).

This system was fully exploitable up to 6,000 metres of recovery altitude, above which only 4% additional power was added, mainly due to cooling.

Pilots generally limited the use of this system to 10 minutes, using it mainly to increase the rate of climb in interception missions: it was, however, only towards the end of the conflict that the MW 50 system became available.

This system could be mounted on different engines.

From the D version, the G and H versions were derived, specific versions for use on bombers: as was the case for the A and B versions, their main difference was given by the opposite direction of rotation, right for the G and left for the H.

- This was followed by the E version which was a conversion of the D-2 with the supercharging specially calibrated for high altitude flight.

Take-off power did not undergo significant increases while cruising power increased by 100 hp (74.5 kW) and combat power, in the high-powered models, by 150 hp (112 kW). The E version was also used as the basis for the R.

This version was fitted with a more powerful and complex two-stage, four-speed supercharger.

Continued improvements to the E model led to the F version. On paper the performance of this new version was supposed to be significantly improved with power rising to 2,400 hp (1,790 kW).

The F model was intended for use on the later versions of the FW 190, but the war ended before production began.

Many tests were conducted to experiment with the use of turbochargers on the 801 engines.

The first was driven by engines of the D version: thus modified it was renamed BMW 801J.

This engine provided 1,810 hp (1,350 kW) at takeoff and 1,500 hp (1,119 kW) at 40,000 feet (12,200 m) altitude.

The increase in available power was also notable: at this altitude, a normal BMW 801D engine could barely deliver 630 hp (470 kW).

The same modification was made to the E version which became the BMW 801 Q: this engine was able to provide, again at 12,200 metres, 1,715 hp (1,279 kW), a power superior to any engine used by the Allies.

Despite their excellent performance, the J and Q versions never entered production for cost reasons.

In their place, projects based on these BMW engines were adopted with different existing engines such as the Junkers Jumo 213.

Fw 190 V

The first prototype, the Fw 190V-1, was powered by a 14-cylinder BMW 139 radial engine with 1,550 hp at take-off, identified by the serial number D-OPZE, and made its maiden flight on 1 June 1938 under the control of Focke Wulf chief test pilot Hans Sander, who declared:
"In my career I have flown many airplanes, but I cannot remember any that impressed me more than the Fw 190, docile and easy to handle from the first flight."

It was armed with a 7.92 mm MG 17 machine gun on the engine and two 13 mm MG 131 machine guns at the wing roots.

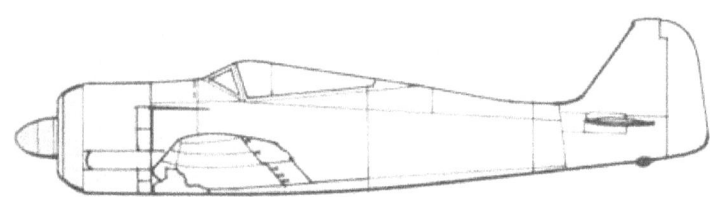

Fw 190V-1 after modifications.

The aircraft had light controls and was well balanced, with an excellent rate of turn, although inferior to that of the Spitfire, the champion in this field, and incredible acceleration.
It was also appreciated for the robustness of its undercarriage, with a wide track and retractable inwards.
The engine was equipped with an annular nose cone, which was supposed to help cool the engine: this solution immediately proved to be inefficient, as the cylinders overheated dangerously, and the passenger compartment filled with smoke, in addition to reaching temperatures of around 60°, so much so

that Sanders stated that he felt like he was holding his feet like two steaks on a grill.

- **V2**

The second V-2 prototype was similar, and was used in performance tests with the modified first prototype, to verify the aerodynamic characteristics with and without the ducted propeller.
It was armed with two MG 17 machine guns on the engine cowling and two MG 131s at the wing roots.
It was also equipped with a Revi 12C collimator and explosive charges for emergency detachment of the canopy.

- **V3 and V4**

The two subsequent prototypes V-3 and V-4 were originally intended to be completed with the BMW 139 engine, but when development of the latter was abandoned, their construction was halted, with the former being used as a source of spare parts, while the Fw 190V-4 was completed with only the airframe for static robustness testing.

- **V5**

The Fw 190V-5 was built to accommodate the new BMW 801 C-0, a 1,600 hp 14-cylinder radial engine, which was larger and heavier than its predecessor, although more powerful, and to balance the increased weight the cockpit had to be moved further back, compromising the aircraft's visibility during ground maneuvers.
The engine was cooled by a ten-bladed fan, which rotated three times faster than the propeller shaft.

The increase in weight created the need to increase the size of the wing to restore the original flight characteristics, and the V-5, after a landing accident, was fitted with the new 18.30 m $^{2\ wing}$ which, although it caused a loss of 10 km/h in terms of speed, made the aircraft more maneuverable and with a faster rate of climb.

With this new configuration the aircraft was called V-5g, while the previous configuration was designated V5k.

Fw 190 V5K.

Fw 190 A

A-0

The first two examples of the planned 40 A-0s rolled off the assembly lines in October 1940 and were given the distinctive prototype designations: Fw 190V-6 and Fw 190V-7.
- Like the next seven examples, they still featured the small wing, as the first nine airframes were in an advanced stage of construction when it was decided to adopt the larger wing.

The latter was adopted starting from the W.Nr. 0015, together with a larger horizontal fin.
From November 1940, the new BMW 801C-1 version of the engine was adopted from model W.Nr. 0010, replacing the pre-series C-0 version.
Six examples, including W.Nr. 0013, 0014, 0018, 0021 and 0022, were delivered in March 1941 to Erprobungsstaffel 190, commanded by Captain Otto Bahrens, which was formed to develop the aircraft for operational use.
The unit was also assigned technicians from Rechlin, and initially operated directly from the Rechlin-Roggenthin airport, before moving to Le Bourget airport in Paris. The RLM commission arrived at this base to force a halt to the program in order to resolve the numerous reliability problems that had arisen, mainly attributable to the propulsion system.
After approximately 50 modifications, the program continued, and production of the A-0 ended after the 28th example (W.Nr. 0035) was completed to make way for the A-1 version, the first production version.
In the small series of A-0s, some aircraft had special features, such as:

- Fw 190V-6 (W.Nr. 0006), sixth prototype and first example of the A-0 series, was used for tests on characteristics and performance.
- Fw 190V-7 (W.Nr. 0007), the seventh prototype and second example of the A-0 series, carried a heavier armament, consisting of two 20 mm Rheinmetall-Borsig MG FF cannons, in addition to the four original 7.92 mm MG 17s, which was tested at Tarnewitz.
  Pending the availability of the MG 151 cannon synchronization system, this armament became the standard for the A-1 version.
- Fw 190V-9 (W.Nr. 0022, code SB+IE), was used to test in Langenhagen, under the direction of Hans Sander, a model of an ejection seat by means of an explosive charge, but the modification was not followed up.
  It was also used to test the armament of four 50 kg SC 50 bombs mounted under a fuselage mount and another four mounted in pairs under the wings.

Fw 190 A-0

A-1

The first production Fw 190A-1 left the Marienburg factory in June 1941, while operational trials with earlier examples continued at Le Bourget airfield.

From the following August, about 30 examples were rolling off the line each month. Deliveries of the examples built by Arado in Warneminde began that month, those built by AGO in Oschersleben in October, and by the end of that month, all 102 examples planned had been produced.

Compared to the pre-production A-0s, only minor modifications had been made, dictated by the intensive testing program at Rechlin-Roggenthin to which the first examples of the aircraft had been subjected.

In early August 1941 the A-1s were distributed to II/JG26.

- It had been necessary to add a system of explosive cartridges to the canopy to allow it to be released in an emergency at speeds above 400 km/h.

The installation of the 20 mm MG 151 cannon was not yet complete, so the armament remained with two MG 17s at the wing roots with another two MG 17s in the fuselage, over the engine.

To increase firepower, two slow-rate-of-fire (51 rounds per minute) 20 mm MG FF cannons were installed outside the carriage mounts.

Armor was installed to protect the cockpit, fuel tanks, and oil tank.

The first examples were delivered to 6/JG26, and by early September 1941 the entire II/JG26 based at Morseele, Belgium, had abandoned its Messerschmitt Bf 109E-7s and been re-equipped with the 190°-1.

A few A-1s were sent to the Russian Front in November 1941, but it took nearly a year for the aircraft to be widely adopted on that front, because Russian fighters were considered inferior to British fighters, and the first units to be equipped with the best German fighter were, therefore, those destined for the Western Front.

Some A-1s, as well as some A-0s, experimented with the FuG 25 IFF device, added to the FuG 7 radio.

Focke-Wulf Fw.190 A-1 W.Nr 033 Moorsele 1941.

A-2

The first A-2s appeared in October 1941, immediately distinguishable by the presence of two 20 mm MG 151 cannons, which replaced the Mg 17s at the wing roots: the only significant structural modification consisted of a further strengthening of the undercarriage.
The 190 was now produced simultaneously by the FW works in Marienburg, the AGO in Oschersleben and the Arado in Warnemünde, so that between October 1941 and July 1942 as many as 952 A-2s entered the Luftwaffe inventory.

- It was powered by a 1700 hp BMW 801C-2 at take-off, and the two MG 17s at the wing roots had been replaced by two 20 mm MG 151/20E cannons with 200 rounds.

The new weapon had necessitated a bulge in the access panel above the wing.

- The new engine offered increased power for one minute in emergency situations, and in combat the maximum speed was 659 km/h at 7,000 metres.

The Revi C/12D reflecting collimator was also introduced to replace the previous Reci C/120, and the electric retraction system of the landing gear was improved.
The changes introduced brought the empty weight to 3,850 kg.
In November 1941 II/JG26 began the transition to this type, transferring its A-1s to the Geschwaderstab.
JG26 was fully equipped with the Fw 190 by early in the new year.
Approximately 420 Fw 190A-2s were built until the winter of 1942.

On a cold day in December 1943, Fw-190A2 'Yellow 16' took off from Herdla airfield in Norway, only to experience engine trouble shortly thereafter. The pilot, left with no other option, made an emergency landing on the water near Solsvika, west of Bergen. This event marked the beginning of a long underwater sleep for Yellow 16, which would not see the light of day for nearly 63 years. On 1 November 2006, a dedicated team brought the aircraft back from its watery grave in a meticulous recovery operation, lifting it from 60 metres below the surface.

A-3

From the winter of 1942 the Fw 190 was produced in the A-3 version, powered by the improved BMW 801D-2, with 1,730 hp at take-off, obtained thanks to a higher compression ratio and a two-speed supercharger with higher pressure.

Fw 190 A3.

This had forced the adoption of C3 fuel, with 96 octane petrol, in place of the previous B4, with 87 octane petrol.

- Engine cooling had finally been improved, with the introduction of three vents on each side of the engine cowling: some A-1s and A-2s undergoing overhaul were also modified.

- The symmetrical engine access panels had been slightly modified in shape, and were equipped with stronger hooks. The armament was the same as the A-2.

JG26 and JG2 on the Channel Front were equipped with this aircraft, although the limited number of aircraft available forced III/JG26 to revert to the Bf 109F.

The Fw 190A-3 was also used to test the aircraft's versatility by transforming it into a fighter-bomber and reconnaissance aircraft.

Following the positive outcome of these, it was planned to massively introduce into the assembly lines a certain number of 'Umrüst-Bausätze' (factory conversion kits) on some examples of the aircraft, traces of which remain of the following:

- Fw 190A-3/U1 a prototype (W.Nr. 130270) with engine mounted 15 cm further forward, a modification adopted by the subsequent A-5 series.
- Fw 190A-3/U2 one example (W.Nr. 130386) armed with the 73 mm RZ 65 unguided missile in two examples under wing pylons.
- Fw 190A-3/U3 a reconnaissance aircraft, equipped with two Rb 50/30 cameras in the fuselage. It was missing the two MG FF cannons.
- Fw 190A-3/U4 reconnaissance aircraft, with two Rb 12.5/7x9 cameras mounted in the rear of the fuselage and an EK 16 or Robot II photo machine gun in the leading edge of the port wing. It also lacked the two MGFF cannons and could carry an additional 300-litre fuel tank in an ETC 501 mount under the fuselage.
- Fw 190A-3/U7 high-altitude fighter, built in three prototypes (W.Nr. 130528, 130530, 130531), equipped with a turbocharger, identifiable by two conspicuous air intakes on the sides of the nose, was armed only with two MG 151 cannons at the wing roots.

In addition to these, many A-3s without a particular designation were adapted to carry an ETC 501 pylon, capable of carrying 500 kg of bombs (one 500 kg SC 500, or two 250 kg SC 250, or

four 50 kg SC 50 with the ER4 adapter) or a 300-liter supplemental tank.
- Some examples also had the two MG FF cannons removed to save weight.

A total of 1,878 Fw 190A-3s were produced by the end of 1942, of which 72, designated Aa-3 (a stood for 'auslandisch', foreign) with the armament of the A-1 and without IFF equipment, were sold to Türkiye.

A-4

The A-4 version, produced in 894 units, was developed from the Fw 190V24 prototype, and flew on 5 February 1942.

It was equipped with a MW 50 water and methanol injection system, which allowed for increased engine power at altitudes below 5,000/6,000 metres and gave the aircraft increased low-altitude performance.

The FuG 7a radio had been replaced by a FuG 16Z or, later, a FuG 25a, and a small brace had been added to the top of the fin, which made it possible to immediately distinguish this version from earlier ones.

The first examples of A-4s were delivered in the early summer of 1942 to the fighter-bomber unit of JG26, shortly followed by the similar unit of JG2, and the two squadrons were employed to counter the landing at Dieppe on 19 August 1942, operating in particular against British shipping, achieving numerous successes.

'Umrüst-Bausätze' conversion kits were also produced for the Fw 190A-4:

- Fw 190A-4/U1, fighter-bomber, with an ETC 501 pylon installed under each wing for one 250 kg SC 250 or one 500 kg SC500 bomb.
  It had only the two MG 151 cannons at the wing root, both the two MG 17s on the engine and the outer MG FF wing cannons having been eliminated.

- Fw 190A-4/U3, fighter-bomber, with an ETC 501 pylon under the fuselage for one 250 kg SC 250 bomb, one 500 kg SC500 bomb or a 300-litre supplementary tank.

It lacked the external MG FF cannons. It was also equipped with additional armour plates.

This sub-version will be followed by the similar F series described later, and will be reclassified Fw 190F-1.

Fw 190 A4/U3.

- Fw 190A-4/U4, reconnaissance aircraft, with two Rb 12 cameras mounted in the rear fuselage and armed with only two 7.92 mm MG 17s in the nose.

- Fw 190A-4/U8, fighter-bomber and reconnaissance aircraft, with full armament could carry four 50 kg SC 50 bombs under the wing pylons (ETC 50) and an additional 300 litre tank under the fuselage.
  By removing the two wing-mounted MG FFs it could carry two 250 kg SC 250 bombs under the wing pylons and an additional 300 litre tank under the fuselage.
  Even eliminating the two MG 17s on the engine, it carried a 250 kg bomb in the fuselage and two additional 300 litre wing tanks.
  This sub-version will be followed by the similar G-series described later.

From the A-4 version the 'Rüstsätze' field conversion kits were also introduced:

- Fw 190A-4/R1 equipped with FuG 16 ZE radio for guiding other fighters in areas beyond radar coverage.
- Fw 190A-4/R6 armed with 21 cm WGr.21 rocket launchers for operations against four-engined bombers.
  This version was supplied to the following units: 1, 2, 5, 11, 26, 51, 54 and 300 Jagdgeschwader and, from 1943, to the two attack wings SG 1 and SG 2 and to SKG 10, the fast bomber wing (Schnellkampfgeschwader).

Reconnaissance examples were supplied to Fernaufklärungsgruppe 123 (strategic reconnaissance unit) and Nahaufklärungsgruppe 13 (tactical reconnaissance unit).

A-5

If the A-4 represented an improvement over the previous variants, the subsequent A-5 demonstrated that the 190 had, by now, definitively overcome all the "illnesses of youth" and had now become a totally reliable vehicle.
The A-5 version, 723 of which were produced between November 1942 and May 1943, replaced the A-4 in April 1943. It featured mounting the engine 6 inches forward to shift the center of gravity.

Focke Wulf Fw 190A-5

Aesthetically it was also distinguished by the cooling fins on the sides of the engine in place of the previous vents, by a small connection at the root of each wing, by the larger and differently designed inspection panel on the left side of the fuselage and by the greater length of the access panel to the two MG 17s in the fuselage in front of the front locking hooks.
Other than the greater number of conversion kits available, it was otherwise similar to the A-4.
The 'Umrüst-Bausätze' kits adopted by the A-5 include:

- Fw 190A-5/U2, long-range night fighter-bomber, equipped with anti-dazzle blades on the exhaust pipes, heated windows and two twin searchlights on the left wing edge: it carried two 300-litre supplementary wing tanks and a 250 kg bomb under the ETC 250 pylon in the fuselage.
  It was armed with only two 20 mm MG 151 cannons at the wing roots.
  Eight examples were certainly built, including W.Nr. 783, 1449, 1450 and 1482, but it cannot be excluded that production was higher and in any case assigned entirely to SKG 10.
  It was later reclassified Fw 190G-2N.

- Fw 190A-5/U3, fighter-bomber, equipped with additional armor, tropical filters and sand sheaths for the weapons, capable of carrying, in various combinations under the fuselage or wing pylons, 1000 kg of bombs or additional tanks. It was armed only with the two MG 17s in the fuselage and two MG 151s at the wing roots. It was later reclassified Fw 190F-2.

- Fw 190A-5/U3 Trop, fighter-bomber based on the A-5/U3, with sand filter for the engine, sand sheaths for the weapons and armoured undercarriage cover.

- Fw 190A-5/U4, reconnaissance (project only), carried two Rb 12 cameras in the rear fuselage.
  It had no wing cannons but only the two 7.9 mm MG 17s in the fuselage.

- Fw 190A-5/U8, fighter-bomber reconnaissance, carried two 300-litre wing supplementary tanks and a 250 kg SC 250 bomb under the ETC 250 pylon in the fuselage.

It was armed with two MG 151s at the wing roots. It was later reclassified Fw 190G-1 and G-2.

- Fw 190A-5/U9, fighter, built in two prototypes (W.Nr. 812 and 816) which will be used for the development of the A-7, A-8 and F-8. It adopts the new wing of the Fw 190A-6.
  The 812 is armed with two 13 mm MG 131s in the nose and two 20 mm MG 151s in the wing roots, the 816 with two MG 131s in the nose and four in the wings.

- Fw 190A-5/U10, fighter, built in a single prototype (W.Nr. 861), used for the development of the subsequent A-6 series with new strengthened wings.
  It was armed with two MG 131s in the nose and four MG 151s in the wings.

- Fw 190A-5/U11, fighter, built in a single prototype (W.Nr. 1303), used for the development of the A-8/R3, F-3/R3 and F-8/R3 sub-versions.
  In place of the external cannons, two containers with a 30 mm MK 103 cannon each are mounted.

- Fw 190A-5/U12, fighter, built in two prototypes (W.Nr. 813 and 814), used as the basis for the A-6/R1.
  In place of the external cannons they mounted two WB 151/20 containers with 2 MG 151s each.

- Fw 190A-5/U13, fighter-bomber, built in a single prototype (W.Nr. 815).
  It was armed only with two MG 151 cannons at the wing roots. It carried a ventral ETC 501 pylon and two 300-litre wing tanks. It was later reclassified Fw 190G-3.

- Fw 190A-5/U14, torpedo bomber, built in two prototypes (W.Nr. 871 and 872). It was armed only with the two MG 151 cannons at the wing roots.
It carried an LFT5b torpedo slung from a ventral ETC 502 mount, which required the adoption of an elongated rear landing gear leg.

- Fw 190A-5/U15, torpedo-launching, like the U14, but with the Blohm & Voss LT950 torpedo.

- Fw 190A-5/U16, fighter, built in one prototype (W.Nr. 1346), armed with the two MG 17s in the nose, the internal MG 151 cannons and two wing containers with 30 mm MK 108 cannon.

- Fw 190A-5/U17, fighter-bomber, armed with two MG 17s in the nose and internal MG 151 cannons.
It had ETC50 underwing mounts (for 50 kg SC 50 bombs) and a ventral ETC 501 mount.
It had a one-piece, armoured undercarriage cover: it was later reclassified Fw 190F-3.

For the A-5, the 'Rüstsätze' R1 and R6 field conversion kits were available, equivalent to the homonymous ones for the A-4 version.

A-6

The increased weight that the Fw 190 had to endure, as a consequence of the multiplicity of roles that had been assigned to it, led to the development of the A-6 series, which had the internal structure of the wing redesigned, specifically for the purpose of bearing the increased weight.

Fw 190 A6.

Production of the A-6 began in May 1943 and ended the following December with 3,223 units leaving the factories.

- The main innovation introduced by this version is a new reinforced wing, already tested on the A-5/U10, which allows the replacement of the two old MGFF cannons with the much more powerful MG 151s, so the armament is now standardized on four wing-mounted MG 151s and two MG17s in the fuselage.

Among the external modifications, the new doors on the wing intrados stand out, with relative ducts for the expulsion of the shell casings for the external weapons, a machine gun on the left wing leading edge and, finally, the adoption of the circular antenna of the radio direction finder on the belly of the fuselage.
The Fw 190A-6 was designed for use on the Russian Front, and was made highly versatile by the quantity of 'Rüstsätze' and 'Umrüst-Bausätze' it was able to accept.
By the end of 1943, Arado, AGO and Fieseler had produced 569 examples of this series, mostly adapted to the 'Rüstsätze' R1 and R6 and used on the Western Front to counter Allied heavy bomber raids in the role of 'Pulk-Zestörer' (destroyer of bomber formations).
The following 'Rüstsätze' field conversion kits were available for the A-6:

- Fw 190A-6/R1, like the Fw 190A-5/U12 from which it was derived, i.e. armed with two WB 151/20 ventral pods with two MG 151 cannons each, in place of the external wing cannons.

- Fw 190A-6/R2, a prototype planned with the new BMW 801TS or BMW 801S-1 engine with turbocharger, and pending its availability a normal BMW 801D-2 with GM-1 injection is used.
  Armed with two underwing containers each with a 30 mm MK 108 cannon, it has no retinue.

- Fw 190A-6/R6, with two 21 cm WGr.21 rocket launchers under the wings, without the external cannons.

- Fw 190A-6/R11 or Fw 190A-6/Neptun: night fighter equipped with FuG 217J Neptun radar system with 18 antennas, placed above the wings, under the wings and in the fuselage.

It also had anti-glare fins for the engine exhausts and heated windows.

It carried an ETC 501 ventral pylon for a 300-litre supplementary tank, and the external guns were sometimes removed to save weight.

A-7

At the end of 1943 the A-7 version was put into production, produced in very limited numbers, according to various sources only about seventy in total.

Focke-Wulf Fw 190 A-7 of JG26 based at Boissy-le-Bois in northern France between Paris and Rouen, 1944.

The models of this series came out of the Focke Wulf, AGO and Fieseler factories.
- For the first time, the now useless 7.92 mm MG 17 machine guns were replaced with the more powerful 13 mm MG 131.

The adoption of the new weapons brought:
- A modification to the access panel to the same, which was more rounded.
- The pitot tube was moved further towards the right wingtip.

- The Revi C-12D collimator was replaced with the Revi 16B.
- The tail wheel was modified.

At least half of the machines produced were of the Fw 190A-7/R2 Zerstörer sub-version, while others were A-7/R6 Pulk-Zerstörer.

The following 'Rüstsätze' field conversion kits were available for the A-7:

- Fw 190A-7/R1, heavy fighter, one example armed like the A-6/R1, with WB 151 canisters for two 20 mm MG 151s.

- Fw 190A-7/R2, heavy fighter, with two 30 mm MK 108 cannon installed in place of the external guns.

- Fw 190A-7/R6, also armed with 21 cm WGr.21 rocket launchers. 40.8 kg of explosive warhead could destroy or damage multiple bombers, if they flew in close formation. The rockct projectile had a timed fuse, set to explode about 1,000 meters from the launch point. The weapon had no "assisted targeting" system, nor did the rocket projectile have any "automatic" or "guided" search for the enemy bomber.

In practice, the WGr. 21 was fired like a common infantry mortar, and had a generally curved trajectory, with a vertical variation of about 40 metres: for this reason, the rocket launcher tube was mounted at an angle of +15° upwards.

The rocket launchers always fired in pairs or "salvos"; therefore the single-engine fighters, which mounted only two W Gr. 21s, had only one shot available.

- Fw 190A-7/R7, heavy fighter, with the canopy strengthened by additional armoured glass panels.

A-8

From January 1944, the A-8 version entered production, which differed from the previous one mainly for the widespread adoption of the MW 50 super-power device, with a 118-litre cylindrical tank placed on the rear of the fuselage, which, in an emergency, could be used as a fuel tank, or removed for the benefit of the GM1 super-power device.
- The adoption of this tank led to a shift in the aircraft's centre of gravity, to rebalance which the ETC 501 pylon was also moved under the fuselage, which was positioned 20 cm further forward.

The aircraft was also equipped with the FuG 16 ZY radio system, which used a Morane-type antenna placed under the left wing: the FuG 25a IFF device was inherited from the previous version, but was often removed from examples operating on the Eastern Front.
- The pitot tube had been moved further towards the right wingtip.

From 1944 onwards, fighter production was increased to cope with the ever-increasing incursions of Allied four-engined aircraft, to the detriment of other specialities, and the Fw 190 was produced in all Focke Wulf factories, such as Cottbus, Sorau and Poznan (the latter in Poland).

The production license was also extended to Dornier, which produced the aircraft in its factory in Wismar: smaller factories contributed to the production effort by manufacturing components, which were sent to the final assembly lines following efficient coordination plans.

Total production of A-8s could thus reach 1,334 units.

Fw 190 A8.

This variant also gave rise to numerous sub-versions, such as the A-8/R1, the A-8/R2, the A-8/R3 with two underwing MK 108 cannons, an unused A-8/R6 and, finally, the A-8/R7 and the A-8/R8, the first with additional external armour on the roof and sides of the cockpit, the second which is essentially made up of the union of the R2 and R7, to which must be added the elimination of the MG 131s, whose recesses on the engine cowling are closed by means of faired covers.

- Also based on the A-8, a small number of examples were produced as an all-weather fighter variant, the A8/R11, with a PKS 12 autopilot, canopy de-icing system, artificial horizon and FuG 125 "Hermine" zero-light orientation system, as well as the A-8/Neptun, equipped with a FuG218 IIIJ radar.

The A-8 fighter corresponds to the F-8 assault, with four ETC5O, ETC71 underwing and ETC501 ventral, which also appears in the form of the F-8/U1, with ETC503 underwing mounts for 300-litre tanks, and which uses the Panzerblitz 1 and 2 anti-tank rockets in 1944/45 and the F-8/R3 with two 30 mm MK-103 underwing in faired containers and elimination of the external MG 151s.

The G-8 also appears, with armament reduced to two MG 151s at the wing root and underwing Mtt. (two 300-litre tanks) or Fw. (two tanks or two 250 kg bombs) attachments.

Luftwaffe gunners load 210mm WfG.21 rockets into the underwing launch tubes of an FW 190 A-8 before a mission against Allied heavy bombers. An additional 300-litre drop tank is also visible under the fuselage. The steel tubes offered considerable drag and degraded the aircraft's performance, but the rocket's 40kg explosive warhead was a powerful anti-bomber weapon. Later versions of the WfG 21 were fitted with quick-release pins.

A-9

The last version of the A series built was the A-9, which was initially intended to be powered by the new 2,400 hp BMW 801 F engine, but this was never produced in time, so the examples produced were fitted with the 2,000 hp BMW 801 TS, and a new cooling fan with 14 blades instead of 12 was also installed.

- This engine was equipped with a more efficient radiator and two larger annular oil tanks, protected by armour that had been increased from 6 to 10 mm.

Initially, this version was to be equipped with a new wooden propeller, but then the majority of the examples produced were equipped with a metal VDM propeller, like the one installed on the previous series.

Aesthetically, the A-9 version was also distinguished by the adoption of a new bubble canopy like that of the Fw 190F-8 series. The armament was similar to that of the A-8 series, but the external wing MG 151 cannons were often removed.

The Fw 190A-9 was produced from the autumn of 1944 in parallel with the A-8, which it did not replace due to the lack of available BMW 801 TS engines.

- The subsequent A-10 series, which was finally supposed to adopt the BMW 801 F, never saw the light of day due to the end of the war.

Fw 190 B and C

The Fw 190A was paired with a fighter with more advanced high-altitude characteristics: development proceeded, starting from early 1943, on three different models:
- The Fw 190B, which still had the BMW 801 radial engine and wing area increased by 11%.
- The Fw 190C, equipped with the Daimler-Benz DB603 in-line engine, was 140 kg lighter than the BMW 801.
- The Fw 190D, with Junkers Jumo inline engine.

For the Fw 190B, only a few aircraft (apparently six) were used, the first three of which were Fw 190A-3/U7, also identified as B-0.
This aircraft was similar to the Fw 190A, with the addition of a nitrous oxide fuel system (GM 1) to increase power at high altitude, fitted only to the fourth aircraft, the installation of a cockpit pressurization system, with double glazing, armament limited to two wing-mounted cannons and an increased wingspan.
- It was powered by the BMW 801TJ radial engine.

A further B-0 was built, followed by a B-1, both equipped with the GM 1 device.
The V-45 and V-47 prototypes of the B-1 series were then built, without a pressurized cabin but with a GM 1 system and BMW 801D-2 engines.
- The Fw 190B was, however, abandoned due to its disappointing performance and unreliable cabin pressurization.

During 1942 and 1943, further prototypes were produced for the development of the Fw 190C high-altitude fighter: the first three, V-13, V-15 and V-16, had a DB 603A-2 engine and lacked a pressurized cabin and turbocharger.

The latter (a DVL TK 11) was fitted to the V-18 prototype, which had a DB 603A-1 engine, take-off power of 1,750 hp, 1,850 hp at an altitude of 2,100 metres and 1,625 hp at an altitude of 5,700 metres.

From 10 December 1942 this prototype, designated V-18/U1 "Kanguruh" (Kangaroo), was delivered to Daimler-Benz for testing.

- The aircraft was tested with the MW-50 and GM-1 boost systems.

Using the MW-50 increased engine power from 1,800 to 2,250 hp on the ground and from 1,630 to 1,900 hp at 5,500 meters altitude.

With the GM-1, injecting 3.5 kg of nitrous oxide per minute in "normal" mode, the power at an altitude of 8,500 meters was 1,500 hp, and with the injection of 7 kg/min in "emergency mode" the power increased to 1,490 hp at an altitude of 9,900 meters.

- Starting in March 1943, the V-29, V-30, V-31, V-32 and V-33 prototypes of the high-altitude fighter were built, also equipped with the pressurization system, as well as DB 603S engines and TK11 turbochargers positioned under the fuselage.

During tests, carried out in 1943 and the first months of 1944, the aircraft demonstrated that it was capable of reaching altitudes above 12,000 metres, but the aircraft showed several development problems, mainly attributable to the turbocharger.

The armament of the Fw 190C was similar to the previous versions of the series: two 7.92 mm machine guns and a pair of

20 mm cannons always equipped with ammunition strips of high-explosive fragmentation shells for air combat. In addition, the Fw 190 C had a unique appearance: an elongated cowling, a four-bladed propeller, long exhaust pipes on the sides and a cowling with a large air intake.

Fw 190C - Prototype V18.

The excellent performances that the Fw 190D, developed in parallel, was capable of achieving, however, led to the abandonment of further developments of the Fw 190C.

Fw 190 D

The 190D "Dora" represents the evolution of the A series into a fighter with a Junkers Jumo 213 12-cylinder, liquid-cooled inline engine, capable of guaranteeing better performance at medium-high altitudes, the Achilles heel of the BMW engine.

This fighter can be considered the best of the various series, excluding the subsequent Ta 152 which, however, was built in negligible quantities.

The Fw 190D was born to respond to the potential threat of the Boeing B-29, which the Germans knew was about to enter service, capable of operating at high altitudes, at which the Fw 190A found itself in serious difficulty, especially if forced to face a large escort of fighters.

- Engineer Kurt Tank was convinced that the BMW radial engine could never achieve the necessary performance at high altitudes, so he turned to the development of an aircraft powered by an inline engine.

Tank's preference was certainly for the Daimler-Benz DB 603 engine, but this engine was opposed by the RLM, mainly for political reasons, and Focke Wulf was pushed to use the Junkers Jumo 213 engine or to remain with the BMW radial: a version with the Daimler engine was, however, studied, but with a low level of priority.

The development of the aircraft then proceeded in several directions: the Fw 190B was born, powered by a BMW 801 equipped with a turbocharger, the Fw 190C, equipped with the DB 603, and finally the Fw 190D equipped with the Jumo 213 engine.

The first two models were plagued by numerous problems and never entered production, and development therefore concentrated on the Fw 190D, although Tank continued to prefer the DB 603 engine which he believed to have superior performance at altitude and greater development potential.

- However, this engine would not have been immediately available, so Tank, while waiting for his favourite engine, which would however only be mounted on the superlative Ta 152, devoted himself to the "Dora", which he saw as a temporary solution.

Despite these less than positive premises, the fighter soon proved to be a true thoroughbred, which in other times would certainly have allowed the Luftwaffe to regain air supremacy over the Allies.

FW 190 D9 WNr. 400616, formerly flown by Uffz. Koch of the famous JG 54 "Greenhearts". This is one of only two surviving FW 190 D9s in the world with an authentic serial number. The aircraft even features the original Jumo 213A previously used on this serial number.

Aesthetically it was quite similar to its predecessor, as the radiator was installed in front of the engine, making it vaguely resemble a fighter powered by a radial engine, albeit more streamlined.

The increased length of the nose required the insertion of a new 49 cm long constant profile fuselage section before the vertical empennage: the latter was enlarged.

Series production immediately switched to the Fw 190D-9, after only a few D-1s and D-2s had been built: the designations D-3 to D-8 were ignored.

- The aircraft was powered by a Junkers Jumo 213A-1 engine capable of developing 1,776 hp at take-off and 1,600 hp at 6,000 meters.
- With the MW-50 water-methanol injection device, however, it reached a whopping 2,240 hp at zero altitude and 2,000 hp at 3,800 meters.

The superpower could be used in combat for no more than ten consecutive minutes, but the fuel tank allowed for an autonomy of forty minutes.

The armament consisted of:

- Two 20 mm MG 151 cannons at the wing roots with 200 rounds each.
- Two engine-mounted 13 mm MG 131 machine guns with 475 rounds each.
- An under-fuselage mount that could accommodate an additional 300-litre tank or a bomb weighing up to 500 kg.

Initially, the D-9 was equipped with the same canopy as the A series, but after a few examples the more teardrop-shaped canopy of the F series was adopted.

Deliveries of the Focke Wulf Fw 190D-9 began in August 1944, initially to III/JG54.

Once the initial mistrust of the pilots, who considered the Jumo to be a bomber engine, was overcome, the "Dora" soon demonstrated that it had a greater climb and dive speed than its predecessor, and was able to turn more tightly.

With a maximum speed in horizontal flight of 698 km/h at 6,200 meters, with superpower, and with a climb to altitude of:
- 2,000 meters in 2' and 1"
- 4,000 in 4' and 5"
- 10,000 in 7' and 1"

was capable of opposing any Allied fighter.
Its pilots considered it superior to the P-51D Mustang.

A famous example was the aircraft of JG 4 commander Gerhard Michalski, a veteran of the air force, who took part in Operation "Bodenplatte" with this aircraft.

Here are the main variants of the D series:

- Fw 190D-9, main production version, powered by a Junkers Jumo 213A-1 engine of 1,776 hp at take-off and armed with two 13 mm MG 131 machine guns on the engine and two 20 mm MG 151 cannon at the wing roots. Between 600 and 700 of these were produced until the end of the war.

- Fw 190D-10, a version similar to the D-9, from which it differed for the 30 mm MK 108 cannon mounted in the engine and firing through the propeller hub, instead of the two MG 131s.
  Only two examples were built.

- Fw 190D-11, powered by a Junkers Jumo 213F three-stage turbocharged engine and armed with two MG 151 cannon at the wing roots and two 30 mm MK 108 cannon in the outer wing panels: it was missing the two MG 131s.
Seven prototypes were built.

- Fw 190D-12, fighter-bomber equipped with a Junkers Jumo 213F-1 engine of 2,060 hp at take-off, mounted in a more extensively armoured cowling.
It was armed with an engine-mounted 30 mm MK 108 and two wing-mounted MG 151 cannon. It was capable of reaching 729 km/h at 12,000 m. Production began in March 1945, but only a few were completed.

- Fw 190D-13, similar to the D-12, from which it differed in its engine, a Junkers Jumo 213EB, and in the replacement of the 30 mm cannon with a 20 mm MG 151. Only two prototypes were completed.

- Fw 190D-14, version with new Daimler-Benz DB603E or DB603LA engine, remained at the project stage.

- Fw 190D-15, version with new Daimler-Benz DB603EB or DB603G engine, remained at the project stage.

Fw 190F

The F-series versions were built as a result of the success achieved by using the A-series aircraft in ground attack operations.

The F series was conceived from the outset for this role, as a replacement for the obsolete Henschel Hs 123 and Junkers Ju 87 (the legendary "'Stuka"), especially on the Eastern Front.

A request to this effect was made by the RLM in early 1942, with an order for the development of an attack and close support version of the aircraft. The first tests were carried out with an Fw 190A-0/U4 (W.Nr. 0008).

This aircraft was equipped with ETC 50 underwing pylons, capable of carrying a 50 kg SC 50 bomb: following the success of the experiment, development continued apace.

The main problem to be solved was the increased weight to which the aircraft was forced, due both to the bombs and to the additional armour needed for better protection from ground fire.

- This protection was, in fact, positioned to protect the fuel tanks, the engine and the undercarriage against fire from below.

However, the idea of protecting the passenger compartment with additional armour was abandoned, as it would have led to an unsustainable increase in weight and a consequent decline in performance.

For the same reason, the idea of strengthening the chassis was abandoned, simply by increasing the shock absorbers' capacity to absorb impacts by increasing their pressure.

The first versions of the aircraft were modifications of aircraft from the A-3, A-4 and A-5 series, which saw the increase in weight compensated by the removal of part of the armament, generally the two wing-mounted MG FF cannons, a solution that limited the decline in performance.

Fw 190F-8 (Wk Nr 93182). This fighter flew in combat while serving with JG 5 based in Norway. Its last mission was on 9 February 1945.

The Focke Wulf Fw 190F was produced in the following versions:

- **Fw 190F-1**

Subsequent designation referring to the Fw 190 A-4/U3, fighter-bomber version of the A-4, from which it differed in its armament reduced to two MG 17 machine guns in the fuselage and two MG 151 cannons on the wing. Under the fuselage it had an ETC 501 pylon for a 250 or 500 kg bomb or, with the ER 4 adapter, for four 50 kg bombs. 18 of the 30 ordered were built, since in the meantime the subsequent A-5 version had become available.

- **Fw 190F-2**

Subsequent designation referring to the Fw 190A-5/U3, of which 63 were built, some of which in the tropical version (A-5/U3 Trop).

When the decision was made to build the F series, another 271 examples were built, designated from the start as F-2, in both normal and tropical (F-2 Trop) versions.

- **Fw 190F-3**

Developed from the Fw 190A-5/U10, A-5(U11, A-5/U12 and A-5/U17 prototypes. Introduced into service in May 1943, it was built mainly in the F-3/R1 sub-version, with four SC 50 bombs mounted under four ETC 50 pylons (two for each wing) and an ETC 501 pylon in the fuselage for bombs up to 500 kg or an additional 300-litre tank.

It was also built in a tropical version (F-3/R1 Trop).
Only three examples of the Fw 190F-3/R3 were produced, which was armed with two 30 mm MK 103 cannons under the wings, as the A-5/U11 prototype had proven to be too heavy, and, furthermore, the 30 mm cannon had proven to have insufficient penetrating power for the Russian T-34 tanks.
The F-3 was produced in 274 units until April 1944 at the Arado factory in Warnemunde, all equipped with a 1,730 hp BMW 801 D-2 engine.

- **Fw 190F-4**

Not produced, it was to have introduced an improved electric bomb release system and been built in two RüstsätzeR1 (one ETC 501 pylon in the fuselage and two ETC 50 wing pylons) and R3 (two MK 103 wing cannons).
The remainder of the armament consisted of two MG 17s and two MG 151s.

- **Fw 190F-5**

Developed from the Fw 190V-36 prototype, it was to have been powered by the 2,400 hp BMW 801 F engine, but was never produced.

- **Fw 190F-6**

Developed from the Fw 190V-37 and V-40 prototypes, like the previous one (but derived from the A-6 version) it should have been powered by the 2,400 hp BMW 801 F engine, but it had the same fate.

Fw 190F-7

Developed on the basis of the Fw 190A-7, it was abandoned at the end of 1943 in favour of the F-8.

- **Fw 190F-8**

Developed on the A-8 base, it is the sub-version of the F series built in the greatest number: between the F-8 and F-9 approximately 385 examples were produced.
As with the A-8, the two MG 17s on the engine had been replaced by two 13mm MG 131s, while the two 20mm MG 151s remained at the wing roots: from January 1945, ETC 71 pylons were adopted in place of the ETC 50s.
Also for the Fw 190F-8, 'Umrüst-Bausätze' conversion kits were produced:
- The F-8/U1 long-range attack aircraft with two 300-liter supplemental tanks or two SC250 bombs under ETC 503 wing pylons.

- The F-8/U2 long-range torpedo bomber, armed with one BT 200, 400 or 700 torpedo under an ETC 501 or ETC 502 pylon in the fuselage and two 300-litre wing fuel tanks under ETC 503 pylons.
It served as the basis for the Fw 190F-8/R16.
- The F-8/U3 torpedo bomber, armed with BT 1000, 1400 and 1850 torpedoes. It served as the basis for the Fw 190F-8/R15.
- The F-8/U4 long-range night attack aircraft, similar to the F-8/R13.
- The F-8/U5 torpedo bomber. Various 'Rüstsätze' were also planned for this model.
- The F-8/R1 had an additional 115-liter fuselage tank.
- The F-8/R3 was built in small numbers for testing, and was armed with two 30 mm MK 103 cannons in underwing gondolas (like the Fw 190A-8/R3), with 32 rounds per gun, instead of the four ETC 50 wing pylons.
- The F-8/R13 night fighter-bomber, equipped with FuG 25, FuG 16ZY and PKS 12 equipment.
- The F-8/R14 torpedo bomber, with the same radio equipment as the R13, and armed with one LT IB torpedo suspended from an ETC 502 pylon.
- The F-8/R15 torpedo bomber, like the previous one but with a BT 1400 torpedo.
- The F-8/R16 torpedo launcher, with two BT 400 torpedoes on ETC 503 wing pylons or one BT 700 torpedo under the ETC 504 fuselage pylon.

Several weapons were tested with the Fw 190F-8, including the Blohm und Voss BV 246 glide bomb, tested on the example with W.Nr.130975, which had no sequel, the SG 113A, a weapon system that fired rockets vertically by means of two sets of two tubes installed in the wings, which was installed on the prototype Fw 190V-75.

A prototype flew in mid-October 1944, and was subsequently tested on three more aircraft at Tarnewitz starting on 6 December 1944.

A prototype (Fw 190V-69) based on the F-8 was used to test the new X-4 air-to-air missile: it carried two of them mounted under two ETC 715 underwing pylons, and was equipped with the PKS 12 aiming system.

This missile was also tested on the subsequent V-70 prototype, destroyed shortly after, and on three production F-8s (W.Nr.583431, 583438 and 584221).

Three prototypes (V-78, W.Nr.551103, V-79, W.Nr.581304 and V-80, W.Nr.586600), ex F-8, were used to test the new AG140 rocket launcher.

- **Fw 190F-9**

It was based on the A-9, and was powered by the 2,000 hp BMW 801 TS engine, equipped with a cooling fan with 14 blades instead of 12, and a new three-bladed wooden VDM propeller produced by Heine and Schwartz with a diameter of 3.5 metres.

Some examples were fitted with an enlarged vertical fin, which was adopted by the subsequent Ta 152s.

It had a new ETC 504 ventral pylon. Only the R1 conversion kit was produced for this version, and some aircraft were fitted with Panzerblitz rocket launchers.

- **Fw 190F-10**

It was based on the A-10 and had a 2,400 hp BMW 801F engine.

For this version, the widespread use of the increased fin was planned.

The main landing gear wheels were new, enlarged to 74 cm in diameter and 21 cm thick.
Like the A-10, this version never went into series production due to the unavailability of the engine.

- **Fw 190F-15**

Built in a single prototype (V-66, W.Nr.584002) it was supposed to be powered by a BMW 801 TS, but had no follow-up.

- **Fw 190F-16**

Built in a single prototype (V-67, W.Nr.930516) it was similar to the F-8, from which it differed only in the replacement of the FuG 16 radio with the FuG 15.

- **Fw 190F-17**

Remaining at the design stage, intended for naval attack, it was to be equipped with the new TSA 2A collimator.

Fw 190 G

The G series versions were conceived as long-range fighter-bombers and were initially based on the Fw 190A-4/U8, equipped with an additional 300-litre tank under each wing hung from a Junkers-type mount, and an ETC 501 mount under the fuselage for bombs.
To save weight, armament was reduced to two inboard 20 mm MG 151 wing cannons, and this standard would remain unchanged for all versions of the G series.
The Fw 190A-4/U8 were redesignated Fw 190G-1 from 1943.
It is believed that 49 examples were built.

- **Fw 190G-2**

It was based on the Fw 190A-5/U2, U8 and U13, the fighter-bomber variants of the Fw 190A-5.
In this version the two 300-litre wing tanks were hung from two Messerschmitt-type pylons, which were more aerodynamically efficient and allowed for greater speed.
The night-time variant G-2/N, equipped with flame suppressors for the exhausts, also saw the light of day in a few examples.
Some G-2s had a wingtip machine gun installed in the left wing. The approximately 600 examples produced were delivered to Schlachtgeschwader, fighter-bomber units, Kampfgeschwader, bomber units and some Nachtschlacht Gruppen, night fighter-bomber units.

- **Fw 190G-3**

It was based on the Fw 190A-5 and A-6, and entered production in the summer of 1943.

It featured the introduction of new underwing attachments produced by Focke Wulf, capable of carrying both the 300-litre supplementary tanks and up to 500 kg of bombs, although in reality, for weight reasons, the load was limited to one 250 kg bomb under each wing.

Fw 190G3 .

This increased the versatility of the aircraft, which could carry two additional wing tanks and bombs under the fuselage on long-range missions, a 300-litre tank under the fuselage and bombs under the wings on medium-range missions, and a full bomb load on short-range missions.

A night variant of this version also saw the light of day, G-3/N, with flame suppressors on the exhausts and landing lights on the leading edge of the left wing.

Some G-3s were later converted to G-3/R5s with the installation of ETC 50 mounts, two under each wing, making them similar to the F series, more specialized in tactical support.

- **Fw 190G-8**

It was produced alongside the A-8 fighter and F-8 attack aircraft from early 1944.

Although its armament was still reduced to the two MG 151 cannons at the wing roots, it retained the bulge of the MG 131 fuselage typical of the twin versions. Like the latter, it had the pitot tube moved further outward on the right wing.

In addition to the ETC 501 attachment under the fuselage, it was equipped with new ETC 503 wing attachments, more tapered than the previous ones, also capable of carrying a wide variety of loads.

Fully loaded, the G-8 weighed 5,200 kg, and had a range of approximately 1,125 km.

Under these conditions the maximum speed was reduced to about 450 km/h. Some examples were fitted with the F-series bubble canopy, others with flame suppressors for night operations.

As had already happened with the G-3, some examples, towards the end of the war, were converted for tactical support, to meet the increasingly desperate need to stop the advance of the Allied armies, thus supporting the F series aircraft in this role.

This conversion was designated G-8/R5, and consisted of the adoption of four ETC 71 underwing mounts (two per wing) for bombs up to 50 kg.

Fw Ta 152

A development of the Focke-Wulf Fw 190, it differed substantially in the adoption of a high aspect ratio wing and thinner profiles suitable for achieving a higher operational ceiling in order to counter Allied bombers operating at high altitude: B-17 Flying Fortresses, American B-24 Liberators and British Lancasters.

- In reality, this aircraft also proved to be very efficient against Allied escort fighters, especially the P-51 Mustang and Hawker Tempest, achieving several successes.

In fact, since the autumn of 1942, the Germans began to evaluate the threat posed by American four-engine bombers, both the B-17, a threat already present, and the B-29, of which the German intelligence services were already aware.

To intercept these aircraft at high altitude, the performance guaranteed by the Fw 190, especially in the A version with radial engine, was no longer sufficient, and a new fighter was needed, designed from the outset for use at high altitudes.

To meet these needs, the Luftwaffe conceived a two-phase program, the first based on the modification of an existing fighter, the second on the development of an entirely new fighter.

The Fw 190Ra-2 and Ra-3 responded to the first requirement, being derived from the Focke Wulf Fw 190D.

The two proposals were very similar, and the two projects differed mainly in wingspan and armament:

- The FW Ra-2 had a wingspan like that of the Fw 190D.
- The FW Ra-3 had it more extended.

The engine was to be a Junkers Jumo 213E with a two-stage, three-speed turbocharger, capable of providing better high-altitude performance than the 213A in the Fw 190D.
- Both projects featured a pressurized cabin and two injection devices, GM-1 (Nitrate Oxide, for high altitude) and MW-50 (Water and Methanol, low altitude).

The fuselage was the same for both models, and was lengthened compared to the Fw 190D to increase internal capacity.
The cockpit was moved back 40 cm to balance the weight and the surface area of the vertical fin was increased.
Armament consisted of one 30 mm cannon mounted in the engine and two 20 mm MG 151s at the wing roots; the Ra-2 had two additional engine-mounted MG 151 cannons.
For the second requirement, the Fw 190Ra-4D project was foreseen.

It too was largely based on the Fw 190D, however, it was more radically modified with an extensive redesign of the airframe, and featured Kurt Tank's favourite Daimler Benz DB 603 engine. In recognition of Tank's achievements, the RLM had meanwhile decided to grant him the honour of designating his new aircraft with the prefix "Ta" instead of "Fw".

The Fw 190Ra-2 and Ra-3 were considered sufficiently different from their predecessors to receive the new designation, and were therefore redesignated Ta 152 in late 1942.
Tank specifically proposed to name the Ra-2 Ta 152B (B stood for Begleitjäger, escort fighter) and the Ra-3 Ta 152H (H for Hohenjäger, high-altitude fighter).
- The Ra-4D was redesignated Ta 153.

The need not to interrupt the production of previous models led to a significant slowdown in the development of the Ta 152, which was accelerated only starting from the winter of 1944, when the threat of American raids had become tragically real.
It was therefore decided to equip the fighter with the wing initially planned for the Ta 153, which was more aerodynamic, easier to build and capable of carrying more fuel.
- It was thus fitted without further modifications to the Ta 152B, while for the Ta 152H new external sections and new flaps were added to increase its span.

The RLM required these aircraft to be powered by the 12-cylinder Jumo 213E engine in an inverted V arrangement, with a displacement of $35,000$ cm3 but Tank was also allowed to continue development of the Ta 152C, equipped with a DB 603 engine.
The first prototypes of the aircraft saw the light in the summer of 1944, and were the Ta 152H, while the first pre-series Ta 152H-0 was ready in October/November and was without wing fuel tanks: a month later the first Ta 152H-1 was ready, equipped with such tanks.
The Ta 152H-1 was armed with a single 30 mm MK 108 cannon in the engine, with 90 rounds, and two 20 mm MG 151 cannons at the wing roots, with 175 rounds each.

Armor was also installed to protect the driver and engine: the machines built were almost all Ta 152H-1/R11 with all-weather equipment.

- The tank for the MW 50 was installed in the left wing for a total of 70 litres, useful to guarantee about thirty minutes of operation of the system, while the tank for the GM 1 was placed behind the pilot's cockpit, and contained 85 litres for an operating autonomy of about seventeen minutes.

A few dozen H-1s were produced starting in January 1945 at the Cottbus factory before it was occupied by the Soviets.
No fighter group managed to make a complete conversion on the fighter, but several Staffeln used it alongside earlier versions.

- Despite its nature as a high-altitude fighter, this superb aircraft was mainly used for ground attack and base protection of the Messerschmitt Me 262, to protect the jet fighters during the delicate phases of take-off and landing.

The Ta 152H-1 was very pleasant to fly, thanks to its large wing surface, but many were destroyed on the ground by Allied air attacks: some were assigned to the Mistel program.
Kurt Tank himself, while flying a Ta 152H from Langenhagen (near Hannover) to Cottbus, had an encounter with four American P-51 Mustang fighters shortly after take-off: his plane was armed, but out of ammunition.
However, Tank only had to press the MW 50 boost button and open the throttle to quickly leave the American fighters behind in a cloud of blue smoke.
The Ta 152H-1 was powered by a Junkers Jumo 213E-1 12-cylinder in-line engine, capable of developing:

- 1,750 hp at take-off (2,050 hp with MW 50 injection).

- 1,320 hp at 10,000 meters (1,740 hp with GM 1 injection).

The maximum speed was:
- 534 km/h from zero meters (563 km/h with MW 50 injection).
- 748 km/h at 9,000 meters with MW 50 injection.
- 759 km/h at 12,500 meters with GM 1 injection.

Its ceiling was a whopping 14,800 meters with GM 1.
Its initial climb rate was 1,050 meters per minute with MW 50 injection.
The Ta 152B did not see series production because Tank gave higher priority to the Ta 152C with DB 603 engine.
Therefore, only three prototypes were built, equipped with a Junkers Jumo 213E-1 engine, without cockpit pressurization.
The Ta 152C was powered by the Daimler-Benz DB 603 engine, which was lighter than the Jumo, and was otherwise similar to the Ta 152B.
It was considered a heavy fighter (Zerstörer): the first prototype, a rebuilt Fw 190D, flew in October 1944.
The first pre-series Ta 152C-0s began flight tests in December 1944 and January 1945.
The Ta 152C-1 was supposed to be mass-produced from April 1944, but production had barely begun when the assembly lines were taken over by the Allied armies, and the fighter never entered service with the Luftwaffe.
The Ta 152C was powered by a 12-cylinder liquid-cooled Daimler-Benz DB 603LA engine capable of developing 2,100 hp at take-off (2,300 hp with MW 50 injection), 1,750 hp at 9,000 metres (1,900 hp at 8,400 metres with MW 50 injection).
He was armed with:
- One engine-mounted 30 mm MK 108 cannon with 90 rounds.

- Two 20 mm MG 151 cannons at the wing roots with 250 rounds per gun.
- Two state-of-the-art 20 mm MG 252 cannons in the outer wings with 175 rounds per gun.

The maximum speed was:
- 526 km/h at sea level (573 km/h with MW 50)
- 701 km/h at 11,500 meters (740 km/h at 10,000 meters with MW 50).
- The initial climb rate was 930 meters per minute with MW 50, the practical ceiling reached 12,300 meters.

The fighter's wing had a two-spar structure made entirely of wood: the flaps and slotted ailerons had a metal frame with plywood covering.
The oval-section wooden fuselage was also integral along its entire length. A crew of two was arranged forward in a tandem configuration: the single-finned vertical tail was made integral with the fuselage and the horizontal tail was cantilevered. The main landing gear was retracted into the engine nacelles, and in place of the tailwheel it was decided to use what was then considered an unusual nose gear, some experience in the use of which was gained in 1938 on a modified FW-58.

The modified Jumo211F engines, equipped with liquid cooling, were chosen, developing 1,340 hp at take-off with three-bladed propellers.

It soon became clear that even the more powerful 1500 hp Jumo211N, let alone the F, would hardly be able to provide the aircraft with the necessary flight characteristics.

The only way out was to use the latest Jumo213, which produced 1776 hp: however, by the time the first two prototypes were assembled, these engines had not yet passed the full test cycle, and, therefore, the prototypes were fitted with the Jumo211F with a take-off power of 1340 hp each, which used three-bladed wooden VS11 propellers.

A Ta 152, of unknown original registration, recovered from the Danish airport of Tirstrup, was requisitioned by the famous Watson's Whizzers team of the United States Army Air Forces (USAAF) and transferred, as part of Operation Lusty, to the airport of Cherbourg (France).

From here, dismantled and suitably packed, it was transferred to the United States aboard the British aircraft carrier HMS Reaper the following July.

The aircraft is kept, but not on display, by the National Air and Space Museum in Washington: as far as is known, this is the only remaining example of the Focke-Wulf fighter.

A second example, identified as Werknummer 150168, was transferred to the United Kingdom in the summer of 1945 and is recorded as having been transported to Farnborough, where the Royal Aircraft Establishment was based, on 3 August.

This aircraft, reported among a pile of wreckage at the end of 1946, was subsequently lost.

Technical Features

Dimensions and weights

- Length: 10.71 meters
- Wingspan: 14.44 meters
- Height: 3.36 meters
- Wing area   : 23.30 m²
- Empty weight: 3,920 kg
- Max take-off weight: 5,220 kg

Propulsion

- Engine: Junkers Jumo 213 E-1 12-cylinder inverted V liquid-cooled
- Power   : 1,754 hp (1,290 kW)

Performance

Max speed: 755 km/h
Autonomy: 1,215 km
Tangency: 14,800 meters

Armament

- Cannons:
    - ❖ 2 MG 151/20 caliber 20 mm
    - ❖ A 30mm MK 108

Versions

- **Ta 152 A**

It was supposed to be the first version, but it appears to have never left the drawing board; up to 7 cannons were planned, including 1 firing through the propeller hub, two in the nose, above the engine, and four in the wings: two placed at the wing root, two moved further outwards.

- **Ta 152 B**

Version with Junker Jumo 213 engine for high altitudes and ordinary-sized wingspan: no news of development.

- **Ta 152 C**

It was the second version designed for series production. It was equipped with the 2,100 hp (1,566 kW) Daimler-Benz DB 603 engine in the "LA" version equipped with a compressor.
The great length of this engine required a lengthening of the fuselage and an increase in the surface of the tailplanes. The wingspan was also increased to 11 meters.
At least 8 prototypes appear to have been prepared but there is no news of production examples.
The engine also did not go beyond the prototype stage.

- **Ta 152 C-1**

It mounted a 30 mm MK 108 cannon and four 20 mm MG 151 cannons in the engine.

- **Ta 152 C-2**

Same version as the C-1 but with a more powerful radio.

- **Ta 152 C-3**

Same version as the C-1 except for being equipped with 1 x 30 mm MK 103 cannon and 4 x 20 mm MG 151.

- **Ta 152 E**

High-altitude photo-reconnaissance model, with "H" series wings, equipped with the Jumo 213E engine, it was the final version scheduled for production from May 1945, but only one prototype was completed.

- **Ta 152 E-1**

Sub-variant of the "E" model with standard wings.

- **Ta 152 H-1**

The only version produced in a significant number of units, characterized by the armament consisting of a 30 mm MK 108 cannon mounted in the engine and two 20 mm MG 151 at the base of the wings. It incorporated all the solutions studied for the best performance at high altitudes such as: engine equipped with 4 stages for work at altitudes above 10,000 meters, elongated wings, 14.44 meters, and additional tanks in the wings.

Focke Wulf Ta 154

The Focke-Wulf Ta 154 was a twin-engined, high-wing night fighter developed by the German aircraft manufacturer Focke-Wulf in the 1940s.
Designed by Kurt Tank, it represented the answer to the more famous British de Havilland Mosquito, even if it did not manage to have the same weight in the Second World War, as only a few examples were produced and delivered to the only operational unit towards the end of the conflict.

Ta.154V-3 .

With the shortage of skilled workers and strategic materials at that time, the German authorities requested a twin-engine night fighter built almost entirely of wood, with the sole exception of parts of the cockpit, the parts of which were joined with a special glue (TEGO).
Only a few examples were built, as were very few missions entrusted to the Ta 154, due to the continuous raids by the

Allies, who destroyed one after the other the factories that produced this glue.

The first prototype was tested in the second half of 1943 and, in direct comparison, managed to outspeed its competitors produced by Messerschmitt AG and Ernst Heinkel Flugzeugwerke AG.

However, the glue issues were its weak point and, after alternative glues were tried without success, any further development of the aircraft was abandoned.

Despite the few missions it flew, this aircraft made it clear that it would be able to give a great boost to the Luftwaffe.

The surviving Ta 154s, after the cessation of hostilities, were brought to the United States and carefully evaluated.

The Ta 154 was a twin-engine aircraft with tricycle landing gear designed in 1942 by Kurt Tank for the night fighter role.

It was an excellent project despite the limitations imposed by having to use non-strategic materials, capable, at least in theory, of competing with the more famous German night fighters.

Technical Features

Dimensions and weights

- Length: 12.60 meters
- Wingspan: 16.00 meters
- Height: 3.67 meters
- Wing area   : 32.4 m²
- Gross weight: 8,845 kg

Propulsion

- Engine: 2 Junkers Jumo 211R
- Power: 1,500 PS (1,103 kW) each

Performance

- Max speed: 632 km/h at 8,000 meters
- Rate of climb: to 8,000 meters in 14 min 30 sec
- Autonomy: 1,370 km
- Tangency: 10,920 meters

Armament

- Cannons:
  - ❖ 2 MG 151/20 caliber 20 mm
  - ❖ 4 MK 108 30 mm caliber

Hans Hahn

Hans Hahn was born on April 14, 1914 in Gotha, Thuringia.
A good physical athlete, he was enlisted on 1 April 1934 as an officer trainee and became a sergeant on 1 December.
He then attended the war school in Munich from January to October 1935, and in November was transferred to the Luftwaffe for flight training in the town of Celle. Promoted to second lieutenant on 1 April 1936, Hahn was selected to compete in the pentathlon at the Games of the XI Olympiad, held in Berlin that summer, but illness prevented him from participating. After completing basic training he was assigned, on 15 April 1937, to the 4th Squadron of the 134th Fighter Wing (4/JG 134) based at Werl, then transferred on 1 November to the fighter pilot school at Werneuchen as an instructor and, after being promoted to lieutenant on 1 February 1939, to JG 3.
On 11 October 1939, by which time World War II had already begun, Hahn was transferred again, this time to the 2nd Fighter Group of the 2nd Fighter Wing (II/JG2, a unit named in memory of the World War I flying ace Manfred von Richthofen) based at Zerbst/Anhalt.
On 15 December he was appointed Squadron Leader of 4/JG2, while his first two victories, reported in the first flight in which he encountered enemy aircraft, were obtained on 14 May 1940 against two RAF Hawker Hurricanes: in any case, only one victory was confirmed and consequently counted as valid.

- By the time the French campaign ended with the Second Armistice of Compiègne, Hahn had already scored a total of five victories.

Hans Hahn's talent emerged fully during the Battle of Britain, where a constant progression led him to achieve victories number 10 (31 August 1940 with the shooting down of three Spitfires) and 20 (20 September 1940, even receiving the Knight's Cross) which earned him a promotion to Captain and the command of III/JG 2.

- The oak leaves to be added to the Knight's Cross were awarded to him on 14 August 1941 following his 41st victory.

Hahn proved himself by recording his 50th personal success on 13 October 1941, his 60th on 4 May 1942 and his 66th, the last on the Western Front, on 16 September 1942 again against an RAF Spitfire.

Meanwhile, on July 16, he was honored with the German Cross in Gold.

On 1 November 1942 the German flying ace was ordered to change operations and transfer to the leadership of II/JG 54, stationed on the Eastern Front.

- Here, in three months, he achieved 42 victories, distinguishing himself particularly on 30 December 1942, when he shot down five aircraft of the VVS, the Soviet Air Force.

On 1 January 1943 he was promoted to Major and surpassed himself on the 14th of the same month when he shot down 7 Lavochkin La-5 fighters, bringing his total to 86 victories, a number increased to 100 on 27 January.

Having taken over command of III/JG 54, Hahn encountered some Soviet fighters in the skies over Staraja Russa.

In the ensuing combat he managed to shoot down a La-5, scoring his 108th and final victory: in fact, his left wing was seriously damaged in the clash and Hahn had difficulty disengaging from the other fighters, managing, however, to head towards the starting base, which he was unable to reach because the engine of his Bf-109 G-2 overheated, forcing him to land in enemy territory.

Soviet sources claimed that Hahn was shot down by Russian ace Pavel Grazhdanikov of the 169 IAP (169th Fighter Air Regiment), who himself fell in action on 5 April 1943 : in any case, once on the ground, he was captured, imprisoned and convicted of war crimes, being transferred to a maximum security prison in the Steppe until 1950, when he was able to return to Germany.

In his homeland he found work as an employee of the pharmaceutical company Bayer, holding a role in sales to the United Kingdom and France: later, he was also director of Wano Schwarzpulver, a gunpowder manufacturer located near Goslar.

Having retired from private life in 1977, he spent the last years of his life, which ended in Munich due to cancer on 18 December 1982, with his family in southern France.

In total Hans Hahn shot down 108 aircraft in 560 missions; 66 aircraft fell on the Western Front and of these 53 were Spitfires, while of the 42 victories scored on the Eastern Front at least 7 were Ilyushin Il-2 Šturmoviks.

Gerhard Barkhorn

Gerhard Barkhorn was the second greatest flying ace in history after Erich Hartmann, and the only one, together with Hartmann himself, to have shot down more than three hundred enemy aircraft.
He was awarded the Knight's Cross with Oak Leaves and Swords for his exploits in 1944.
- This pilot shot down a total of 301 enemy aircraft in 1,104 combat missions during World War II, serving in the Luftwaffe.

Barkhorn was also the second best German ace on the Eastern Front where he achieved all his victories flying Messerschmitt Bf 109s and Focke-Wulf Fw 190s.
At the end of the conflict he also flew some Messerschmitt Me 262s in Adolf Galland's unit, the Jagdverband 44.
Taken prisoner, after the conflict he joined the German Federal Air Force.
He died in a car accident in 1983.
Gerhard Barkhorn was born on 20 May 1919 in Königsberg, East Prussia. In 1937 he entered the Luftwaffe with the rank of Fahnenjunker, officer cadet, beginning flight training in March of the following year, after which he was assigned to the 3rd Squadron of the 2nd Fighter Wing (3./JG 2).
In August 1940 he was transferred to the 6th Squadron of the II Group of the 52nd Fighter Wing (6./II.JG 52) to take part in the Battle of Britain, without obtaining any victories, being instead shot down twice: one of these times his Messerschmitt Bf 109E was hit by a Supermarine Spitfire in the radiator, and only with great difficulty did Barkhorn manage to retreat towards the base, but on the way he was attacked again and shot down,

having to parachute into the English Channel under the eyes of a comrade of his who alerted the rescue services, who recovered Barkhorn without serious consequences.

Barkhorn's first victory came on his 120th mission, on July 2, 1941, on the Eastern Front: by November 30 the number of victories had risen to ten.

On 21 May 1942 he was appointed squadron leader of 4./JG 52. That month he shot down a total of seven enemy aircraft.

Compared to other German aces, Barkhorn never recorded a high number of victories during a single mission or in a single day (he stopped at four and seven victories respectively), however he gained another sixteen victories in June and thirty-one in July: on the 25th of the latter month he was wounded in combat aboard his Messerschmitt Bf 109F-4.

Now a lieutenant, Barkhorn was decorated with the Knight's Cross of the Iron Cross on 23 August 1942, after achieving 64 personal victories.

After a period of rest, the Luftwaffe pilot returned to the Eastern Front in early October, a month during which he shot down 14 Soviet aircraft, followed by another 7 in November and 17 in December: on the 19th of this month he reached the milestone of 100 victories against a Curtiss P-40.

After five more victories he was awarded the Knight's Cross with Oak Leaves on 11 January 1943. On 1 September of the following year, when he had already become a Captain, he was appointed Group Commander of the 2nd Group of the 52nd Fighter Wing (II./JG 52), a unit which he commanded until 15 January 1945.

Previously, in August, he had shot down another 24 aircraft (on 8 August he reached 150 personal victories with an Il-2 Šturmovik), continuing the streak of victories by adding fifteen in September, twenty-three in November (he reached 200 victories on the 30th of the month, the fifth Luftwaffe pilot to reach this milestone) and twenty-eight in December.

On January 23, 1944, Barkhorn became the first pilot in history to complete 1,000 war missions.

On 12 February he increased his victories to 250, the third Luftwaffe pilot to do so.

His bravery earned him the Swords to be added to the Knight's Cross with Oak Leaves, which he received on 2 March 1944 to reward his 251st victory.

However, these successes were not without risks: Barkhorn was shot down nine times during his career, had to parachute once or twice, and was wounded two or three times.

On May 31, 1944, in fact, he was wounded for the second time by a Soviet Bell P-39 Airacobra during his sixth mission of the day: tired and not very concentrated, the German did not notice the enemy aircraft that strafed his Bf 109G-6, causing him serious wounds to his right arm and leg that forced him to a four-month convalescence period.

Returning to the front at the end of October, he scored his 275th victory on 14 November: his last success, his 301st, was achieved on 5 January 1945 against a Lavochkin La-5.

On 16 January 1943, Barkhorn, who had been promoted to Major, was appointed commander of Jagdgeschwader 6 based in Posen to participate in the defense of the Reich. Still limited by the effects of his wounds, he had to resign from command of the unit on 10 April for a further period of hospitalization. He then joined Jagdverband 44 commanded by Adolf Galland and equipped with Messerschmitt Me 262 jet aircraft.

On 21 April, during his second mission with the new unit, the right engine of his Me 262 failed, forcing him to abort the attack he had begun against a formation of US bombers.

The intervention of two Bf 109s kept away the P-51 Mustangs and Spitfires of the 403rd Canadian Squadron escort, but Barkhorn had to make an emergency landing in a forest clearing: on impact Barkhorn was thrown forward and the canopy, which he had opened to exit the plane more quickly, closed violently, hitting him in the neck, forcing him to be hospitalised again and preventing him from flying again before the end of the war.

Taken prisoner by the Soviets, he managed to escape and ended up in Allied hands, returning free in September 1945.

In 1955 he joined the reborn West German Luftwaffe, completing a refresher course at RAF Valley in Wales. Promoted to Colonel, he then commanded the 31st Fighter-Bomber Wing, rising over time to the rank of Generalleutnant and eventually commanding NATO's Fourth Allied Tactical Air Force at Ramstein.

He retired from the service in 1976.

Gerhard Barkhorn died on January 8, 1983 at the age of 64 after two days in hospital following a traffic accident near Cologne: his wife Christl died instantly in the accident, which was caused by bad weather on the highway.

Heinz Sachsenberg

Heinz Sachsenberg was born on 12 July 1922 in Dessau, Saxony, the grandson of Gotthard Sachsenberg, a World War I ace.
Having enlisted as an officer in the Luftwaffe and after obtaining his war pilot's licence, which he achieved by finishing at the top of his class, he was assigned at the end of 1942 to JG52 which operated on the Eastern Front.
Here on his second sortie he shot down a Russian Il-2 Sturmovik, but his was a continuous escalation so much so that already at the end of 1943 his carnet counted 52 confirmed victories.
In January 1944, however, misfortune struck him: his BF-109, heavily damaged during a dogfight against a Russian fighter, had to make a difficult emergency landing near his airfield, and he had the skill to save himself by exiting the cockpit before the plane exploded.
At this time he already had 72 confirmed victories under his belt, was nominated for the Iron Cross, and received it when he shortly thereafter reached the tally of 101 victories, all officially confirmed.
Once back in the squadron he started to get busy and, shortly thereafter, he had 103 victories but unfortunately he was shot down by a P-51 fighter in the skies over Romania.
He suffered quite serious injuries but Sachsenberg's mettle was not dented, indeed, he returned to fight obtaining his 104th victory. He was given a very important task, transferred to JG7 which was equipped with the 262 jets, he had to establish a team that had a particular load: to protect the 262 on landing.

The Me-262s were first-generation jet fighters with all the trimmings, their worst flaw was that the landing maneuver had to be done with the engine off.
basically had to glide until they touched the runway, making them easy prey for any Allied fighter, since without an engine the airplane was unable to perform even the slightest evasive or disengagement maneuver.
This is where the specially prepared FW 190 D-9 "Dora" were to come into play: providing cover for the 262s and shooting down any kind of threat.
Thus, the JV44 "Papagai" Staffel was formed.
Sachsenberg, after having served in the Papagai which he founded, so much so that it was also called "Sachsenberg Pappagai staffel" and received the highest honours of the Reich, passed away one night on 17 June 1951 due to unexpected complications arising from some war wounds.

www.ingramcontent.com/pod-product-compliance
Lightning Source LLC
Chambersburg PA
CBHW071514040426
42444CB00008B/1643